100 Best Restaurants
IN ARIZONA

(14th Edition)

Comments from Readers . . .

"Your guide is highly regarded by us in the industry."

". . . the most definitive guide to dining in the area."

"Never have I encountered a better publication regarding this subject."

"An outstanding review job."

". . . found your dope very accurate."

". . . take this opportunity to compliment you on the great job you have done."

"It is one of the better guides that I've read, and I found most of your conclusions accurate."

"You're right on the money!"

". . . really a super job!"

"We have agreed pretty closely with your evaluations and descriptions."

"Use your book extensively."

"I am very impressed with your book. . . ."

". . . and will continue to rely on your culinary judgment."

100 Best Restaurants
IN ARIZONA

An economy gourmet guide
to dining out in the Grand Canyon State

By John and Joan Bogert

A. D. M. Company, Inc.
Phoenix, Arizona

14th Edition

Library of Congress Catalog Card No. 77-79784

ISBN: 0-937974-10-2

Produced by:
Arizona Desert Minerals Company, Inc.
P.O. Box 10462
Phoenix, Arizona 85064-0462

Printed in the United States of America

“Come quick, I am
swallowing stars!”
Dom Perignon
French monk on his
invention of champagne

Dear Reader:

After 14 years of reviewing restaurants, writing and publishing this successful guide, we now plan to broaden our horizons in a related field. Accordingly, we seek a responsible party with a wish to take over this established business enterprise.

Published annually since 1978, this popular, gourmet dining guide is displayed and sold in over 150 bookstores and retail outlets throughout Arizona. The potential for continued sales growth is excellent.

We wish to sell 100% ownership, which includes cover artwork, sales records, editorial files, full access to financial history, and our services in an advisory capacity as requested for one year.

For further information contact:

John R. Bogert
Joan N. Bogert
P. O. Box 10462
Phoenix, Arizona 85064-0462

Contents

How to Use This Guide . . .

Publication of this revised, updated 14th edition continues the overwhelming success begun with the first edition published in September 1977. This 14th edition continues to reflect our experiences eating out in restaurants in Arizona for over 300 nights during the past 12 months. It is only domestic and foreign travel that stops our evening pilgrimage to sample and test a new food emporium. Add to this experience another 250 lunches (either together or separately), plus Sunday brunches, and we feel we continue to have a good rounded, multi-faceted view of the Arizona restaurant scene.

This guide is unique because we have recently eaten in each and every restaurant listed herein several times (more than a dozen times in some cases), the owners and restaurant personnel do not know us, we always pay our own bill, and have never taken a free meal, drink, payment or gift of any kind that may influence our judgment. In other words, this is an honest book. We solicit no advertising and are not subsidized by any individual or organization. Regrettably, as you are aware, many other restaurant guides are based on paid advertising and give glowing descriptions of every dining room.

Comments and ratings in this guide basically apply only for dinner (and a special section for Sunday brunches), although we have been influenced by our luncheon experiences. Also, many Arizona restaurants are open *only* for lunch and have not been considered in this book. However, restaurants open for lunch during normal noonday hours have a special note to that effect. Normal lunch hours are considered to be between 11:30 a.m. and 2:30 p.m. Monday through Friday.

Problems for handicapped persons are still noted as a feature of this 1991 fourteenth edition.

With this edition we have added, where possible, the major cross-streets to aid in locating the restaurants.

Success is a many splendored thing. Although somewhat exasperating, we take a certain pride in noting that restaurant managements are among the very first to purchase each of our new editions. Thus, any constructive criticism that we have levied against a certain restaurant is often cause for quick change and improvement. Of course, you, the reader, benefit by this action and we take pride in having prodded the restaurants into doing a better job.

Restaurant enjoyment is enhanced if a few simple rules are followed:

(1) Make a reservation if possible to do so. If you find you cannot keep it, or will be late, telephone and advise them of your change in plans;

(2) Eat no earlier than 7:30 p.m. Few restaurants close before 9:00 p.m., so you have ample time and you avoid the usual crowded period between 6:00 p.m. and 7:30 p.m.;

(3) Always ask the price of any special, off-menu item before ordering. Failure to do so will often mean a pocketbook-shock when the bill is presented;

(4) Saturday evening is the most popular "eating-out" night of the week, followed by Friday and Thursday. To avoid crowds, receive better service, and probably improve your chances of the chef giving greater attention to your order, dine out earlier in the week;

(5) Recognize that the food is often only as good as the chef's current disposition, and everyone has an offday once in awhile;

(6) If you are a non-smoker and tobacco smoke is annoying, when you make your reservation ask to be seated in the non-smoking area. Most restaurants in Arizona now have no smoking areas. However, many restaurants that have not designated a specific non-smoking area are very willing to quickly establish one for you and your party;

(7) Know what credit cards are accepted and save embarrassment scrambling for cash if your little plastic rectangle is not recognized;

(8) Show your pleasure or annoyance with the quality of the food by advising the maitre d', captain or the owner. Show your pleasure or annoyance with the table service by the size of your gratuity—and also advise the maitre d', captain, owner, etc. We have a little rule that seems to work well. When we walk into a restaurant we mentally plan on leaving 10% of the amount on the check (before taxes) as a tip.

As the meal progresses the percentage declines with poor service or rises with good service. We have occasionally left no tip, have rarely left 20%, and estimate our average for some 600 meals over a year at 13%.

Information contained herein continues to be based on our personal visits to the establishments named. The judgments, opinions and editorial comments expressed are solely those of the authors and are for general informational purposes only. All data has been thoroughly checked and is believed to be accurate. But despite our careful attention to detail we cannot be responsible for changes beyond our control. No malice is intended or implied by our comments and/or by the omission of any restaurant in this publication.

Look for continued annual revisions of this guide. There are new restaurants opening up every week and sooner or later we will try them all. The 15th edition of the *100 BEST RESTAURANTS in Arizona* is now being researched. Most certainly many of the current quality ratings will be changed, and some of the top 100 restaurants will be dropped completely. But, of course, there will always be new names and new menus for continuing adventures in good eating in Arizona.

Bon appetit!

John R. Bogert
Joan N. Bogert

A Few More Thoughts . . .

No Smoking Rooms

We make no judgments on the merits or evils of smoking. Suffice it to say that the smell of tobacco is annoying to some people. Because of complaints from patrons, and an obvious attempt to encourage business from those who are allergic to tobacco, a number of restaurants make an effort to provide "no-smoking" areas. This movement was brought to a crescendo on July 1, 1986, when the Phoenix City Council passed Ordinance G2883. This progressive law requires restaurants to either (1) provide a non-smoking area for patrons, or (2) post a visible notice at the entrance stating that the establishment does not provide a non-smoking area.

This legislative action had an immediate positive effect and now an estimated 90 percent of the upscale restaurants in Phoenix provide non-smoking areas. Happily the idea is spreading to Scottsdale, Tempe, Mesa and Tucson. Many public dining rooms in these locales are following the lead of Phoenix by setting aside a special area for non-smokers. During this transition period we have found it virtually impossible to keep up to date with the growing trend. Accordingly, we are dropping this service to readers since it has now become almost a "non-issue."

The Rating System

Everyone has a favorite restaurant and usually the choice is not because of the food only. Food, yes, and most important; but also other factors: the service, the cost, the hospitality of the host, convenience, cleanliness, general appearance and comfort, parking facilities and many other amenities (or lack of them) that make a certain restaurant your special choice.

In order to aid the users of this guide in ranking the *100 BEST RESTAURANTS in Arizona,* we have devised a rating system. It is based on our general, overall impression of the establishment, but gives greatest emphasis to the quality of the food. Next, and of lesser importance, is the service, followed by the cost and finally, the general appearance and comfort. On a numerical basis we weigh these factors as follows:

Quality of Food = 60%
Efficiency of Service = 20%
Overall Cost = 15%
General Appearance and Comfort = 05%

Based on the above factors, we have rated the restaurants included in this guide with a star system as follows:

Outstanding ***
Excellent **
Very Good *

Note: the rating system is a qualitative judgment of restaurants within each group. Thus, a two-star Chinese restaurant is "excellent," compared to *other* Chinese places, but not compared to Italian or French restaurants.

The **star rating** is shown in the upper left-hand corner of each restaurant description page.

Definitions

For the purpose of brevity, at the bottom of each restaurant description page we list essential data on hours, open for lunch, closing days, reservations, parking, credit cards, handicapped access and the **average check for two.** All of this is self-explanatory except the **average check for two.**

It is usually a couple that goes out to eat in a restaurant; often three or four persons, and occasionally five or more. Rarely is it one person. Thus the **average check for two** is the cost of dinner for two persons before tax and **not** including cocktails, wine, gratuities and special services. In most places it includes soup or salad, entree, dessert and beverage.

The abbreviations for credit cards in the guide are:

AE —American Express
CB—Carte Blanche
DC—Diners Club
MC—MasterCard
V —VISA

However, in order to save space under the new format, if a restaurant accepts AE, MC and V this is considered to be "All."

Books are available at discounts in quantity lots for industrial and sales promotional uses. For details write:

A. D. M. Company, Inc.
P.O. Box 10462
Phoenix, AZ 85064-0462

WE WELCOME your comments, suggestions and questions. Please write to:

ADM Company, Inc.
P.O. Box 10462
Phoenix, AZ 85064-0462

Look for the 1992 Fifteenth Edition in your favorite bookstore, or card and gift shop around October 25, 1991.

Allegro

1301 E. Northern Avenue
Phoenix 861-1391

PHOENIX

A small place where the lights are dim, the music soft, service is attentive and a fresh flower graces every table. The accent color is burgundy, offset by living greenery with mirrors giving an expansive feeling — all under a grey and white striped, tent-like ceiling.

Freshly prepared food is stressed and prices are right. The easy to read menu is not overloaded. The 11 pasta dishes range from spaghetti with meatballs or sausage to linguini with red or white clam sauce, and include soup or salad. Try the chef's choice of pasta dishes. They have never disappointed. They offer four chicken entrees, five veal dishes, two beef, two fish, plus lobster tails fra diavolo, scallops, and two scampi dishes. Quality is there. Medallions of veal sauteed with butter, lemon, garlic, wine and capers, are served with pride. Both the scampi Allegro and the sauteed chicken breasts with sherry and tarragon are well handled.

Hot garlic bread and fresh, crunchy vegetables accompany every meal, as well as a choice of soup del giorno or an above average dinner salad. The creamy Italian dressing with a hint of anchovy makes the salad. The homemade cheesecake is the best dessert. Table service is professionally competent.

- **HOURS: Sun. thru Thurs.: 5:30 p.m.–10:00 p.m.**
Fri. and Sat.: 5:30 p.m.–10:30 p.m.
Open for lunch
- **CLOSING DAYS: None**
- **RESERVATIONS: Yes**
- **PARKING: Lot**
- **CREDIT CARDS: All**
- **HANDICAPPED ACCESS: No difficulty**
- **AVERAGE CHECK FOR TWO: $30.00**

Ambrosino's

2122 N. Scottsdale Road
Scottsdale 994-8404

SCOTTSDALE

An imposing statue of Caesar and six maidens welcome you to romantic Italy. Dining is usually confined to the Emerald Green Room where mirrored walls give an expansive feeling while maintaining intimacy.

Of dependable excellence, the menu includes gourmet pastas, a well-rounded selection of veal and chicken dishes, steaks, rack of lamb, and a long list of fish and seafood entrees. We give high praise to the spinach tortellini verde stuffed with veal, chicken and prosciutto in Alfredo sauce with walnuts and fresh mushrooms, chicken Genovesa with eggplant and creamed spinach, veal Francaise sauteed in Marsala wine with Amaretto and served with broccoli, and the shrimp de Jonge with seasoned bread crumbs, garlic and butter. The veal saltimboca is probably the best in Arizona.

All entrees are served with a family style salad brought pre-mixed to the table. The Italian bread with sweet butter is nice but the toasted garlic bread is outstanding. The ricotta cheesecake with chocolate sauce deserves a medal; the cannoli is fresh made and velvety smooth.

Ambrosino's wine list is excellent accenting Italian vineyards and prices are fair. Table service is winning with black-tied waiters obliging and helpful.

- **HOURS:** **Tues. thru Thurs. & Sun.: 5:00 p.m.–10:00 p.m.**
  Fri. and Sat.: 5:00 p.m.–11:00 p.m.
- **CLOSING DAYS: Mon.** • **RESERVATIONS: 4 or more**
- **PARKING: Lot** • **CREDIT CARDS: All**
- **HANDICAPPED ACCESS: No difficulty**
- **AVERAGE CHECK FOR TWO: $40.00**

* *

Seafood
American

American Grill

6113 N. Scottsdale Rd., Scottsdale 948-9907
1233 S. Alma School Rd., Mesa 844-1918

SCOTTSDALE – MESA

This is Boston at the turn of the century with a large bar, kitchen open to view, a lot of woodwork with brass railings, overhead fans, tile floors and comfortable booths and tables. The mood is casual. Desserts are exhibited on a marble pedestial table in the center of the dining room. The Yankee cuisine with southwest and continental highlights is perfect to behold, to taste, and to enthuse over.

The accent is on chowders, fresh fish and seafood dishes, although the sauteed almond chicken with Arizona citrus sauce is edible poetry. They specialize in chowders and make to order Boston or Manhattan clam chowder, as well as corn and fish chowders, and a crab bisque. Some of the more exciting entrees include grilled swordfish over black bean sauce and salsa fresca, grilled salmon and mahi-mahi over specialty sauces, Cajun blackened rockfish and prime rib, a grilled veal chop, steaks and Sonora barbecued baby back ribs.

With all entrees you receive an outstanding dinner salad plus a choice of an excellent cole slaw with peanuts, little red-skinned potatoes, French fries, fresh seasonable vegetables, macaroni and cheese or a cheese grits casserole. The wine list is all U.S.A. and reasonably priced. The desserts have real elegance.

- **HOURS: Sun. thru Thurs.: 5:00 p.m.–10:00 p.m.**
  Fri. and Sat.: 5:00 p.m.–11:00 p.m.
  Open for lunch
- **CLOSING DAYS: None**
- **RESERVATIONS: Yes**
- **PARKING: Shopping center lot**
- **CREDIT CARDS: All**
- **HANDICAPPED ACCESS: No difficulty**
- **AVERAGE CHECK FOR TWO: $42.00**

The Anderson House

Scottsdale Center
7373 N. Scottsdale Road
Scottsdale 951-1778

SCOTTSDALE

An impressive wood stairway dominates the foyer and leads to second floor dining rooms. Paneling, beamed ceilings and abundant polished wood throughout suggest an exclusive private club. Five dining rooms are all separate and distinct in decor. An aristocratic aura pervades the place. Silverware, crystal, china and table napery are always perfect.

A daily changing menu of wide range promises a gastronomic adventure. Appetizers, soups, salads, entrees and desserts create problems in decision making. The roast prime rib of beef is above average as is the butterflied leg of lamb, marinated, grilled and basted with lemon-thyme butter. The sea scallops with spinach in garlic cream, and the popular chicken and dumplings come over well as do the Caesar and spinach salads, prepared for either one person or two.

All entrees come with a mixed lettuce salad and your choice of five dressings, fresh vegetables, and hot bread. Among the dessert choices the bread pudding, apple and macadamia nut mud pies are yummy. The modest priced wine list shows care in the choosing. Table service is sharp and efficient. The handling of reservations is often sloppy.

- **HOURS: Mon. thru Sun.: 5:00 p.m.–10:00 p.m.**
  Open for lunch
- **CLOSING DAYS: None**
- **RESERVATIONS: Yes**
- **PARKING: Lot**
- **CREDIT CARDS: All**
- **HANDICAPPED ACCESS: No difficulty**
- **AVERAGE CHECK FOR TWO: $40.00**

*

Continental

Anthony's

6440 N. Campbell Ave.
Tucson

299-1771

TUCSON

In the Catalina foothills, boasting magnificent views of the mountains and Tucson's skyline, is an epicure's delight. Picture windows, a massive stone fireplace, and an angled beam ceiling are the high points of the decor. Villeroy and Boch table settings are crisp and tidy. A talented piano player enlivens your evening.

The chef's diversified skills range from a terrine of sweetbreads and Sonoran quesadilla appetizers to Caesar, hearts of palm, and spinach salads to roasted quail Muscat, filet of pork St. Moritz, and lamb noisettes Helder. Standout dishes are the spinach tortellini with prosciutto and pine nuts, the breast of chicken with crayfish and vegetable saffron rice, shrimp scampi and all the steaks. The roast rack of lamb has been too fatty on occasion, and the veal dishes often miss the mark.

With all entrees comes a decent soup du jour or an excellent green lettuce salad with a superior vinaigrette or crumbled bleu cheese dressings. Fresh vegetables served with the entrees vary daily. The warm dinner rolls make no impression. An arresting assortment of fresh baked cakes are available from a pastry cart, and a daily classic souffle is announced by the formally dressed waiter. The wine list is superior and prices are reasonable. Table service is professional and above reproach.

- **HOURS: Mon. thru Sun.: 5:30 p.m.–10:00 p.m.**
  Open for lunch Mon. thru Sat.
- **CLOSING DAYS: None**
- **RESERVATIONS: Yes**
- **PARKING: Lot and valet**
- **CREDIT CARDS: All**
- **HANDICAPPED ACCESS: No difficulty**
- **AVERAGE CHECK FOR TWO: $52.00**

* *Continental*

Arizona Inn

2200 E. Elm Street
Tucson 325-1541

TUCSON

An aura of quiet elegance prevails in this 50-year-old pink adobe inn. The cathedral ceilinged dining room is filled with tables discreetly placed to provide an intimate dining experience for all. When weather permits, request a table on the patio. The view of the lush lawns, shrubbery and colorful flowers will soothe the harried soul.

It is difficult to capture the quality of the changing cuisine with mere superlatives. To begin, the Caesar, garden and special salad du jour are superb. When it is offered, the spinach soup is scrumptious. We have found the roast rack of lamb to be flawless and the tenderloin of pork roasted in sesame seeds, honey and ginger, and the smoked chicken breast with spinach are mouth-watering. The veal cutlet Oscar and the tournedos of beef Rossini are both exemplary.

Meals include relish tray; soup, consomme or tomato juice, salad, vegetable, potato or rice and rolls. The brandied carrots are probably the tastiest vegetables we have ever eaten and the potato baked in duck stock is outstanding. Tempting desserts include apple pie, pecan pie and more. The wine list includes some 40 exemplary labels. A new lighter menu for more modest appetites offers some nice choices. Table service has always been quick and efficient.

- **HOURS: Mon. thru Sun.: 6:00 p.m.–9:00 p.m.**
  Open for breakfast and lunch
- **CLOSING DAYS: None**
- **RESERVATIONS: Yes**
- **PARKING: Lot and Street**
- **CREDIT CARDS: All**
- **HANDICAPPED ACCESS: Ramps; no difficulty**
- **AVERAGE CHECK FOR TWO: $40.00**

Aunt Chilada's

7330 N. Dreamy Draw Dr., Phoenix 944-1286
2021 W. Baseline Rd., Tempe 438-0992

PHOENIX-TEMPE

An ersatz bit of Old Mexico in The Pointe complexes. There are gardens, fountains and fireplaces and cantina dining both inside and outside. They are cute, colorful and quaint with some unique Mexican food items.

The hot taco chips come with a salsa and a hot sauce. Although purists may deplore some of the concoctions and combinations, in most cases they come across well. The Mexican tequila burger is wrapped in a flour tortilla, and be sure to check out the broiled chicken breast in a casserole with chiles, melted cheese and sour cream. Instead of the usual boring Spanish rice, you receive noodles (fideos) with your refried beans. Seafood enchiladas are stuffed with crab, shrimp and whitefish covered with Newburg sauce.

The standard tacos, burros, tostados and chimichangas (choice of chicken or beef) tamales (beef or green corn) and enchiladas are enjoyable and of dependable excellence. There is also carne asada, "sweat hot" chili con carne, and "El Grande Sombrero." This last is a generous sampling of just about everything.

There is no excuse for the paper napkins, but table service is bustling. Music and cocktails are enjoyable.

- **HOURS: Mon. thru Thurs.: 5:00 p.m.–11:00 p.m.**
  Fri. and Sat.: 5:00 p.m.–12 midnight
  Sun.: 5:00 p.m.–10:00 p.m.
- **CLOSING DAYS: None**
- **RESERVATIONS: Yes**
- **PARKING: Lot**
- **CREDIT CARDS: All**
- **HANDICAPPED ACCESS: Three steps in Phoenix**
- **AVERAGE CHECK FOR TWO: $20.00**

Avanti

2728 E. Thomas Rd., Phoenix 956-0900
3102 N. Scottsdale Rd., Scottsdale 949-8333

PHOENIX – SCOTTSDALE

Dedicated attention to details and tastefully appointed tables accented by fresh flowers, palms and original art characterize these two fine restaurants. The decor at Thomas Road is austere Eastern black, white and chrome sophistication with mirrors. The Scottsdale Avanti reflects a Mediterranean atmosphere with white stucco walls and a mini kitchen in one dining room.

The inspired menu, which leans toward Italy, is basically the same in both restaurants. Regrettably, it is white printing on black paper and can be difficult to read. You begin with a delightful hot garlic toast presented soon after the menu. What to choose? After over a dozen visits we have only the highest praise for the many beef, veal, poultry and seafood entrees. Pasta? A mouth-watering pasta list covers all the basic and then some. Undecided? You can't go wrong with the chicken breast Angelo with eggplant and cheeses, the tortellini Portofino with walnuts and mushrooms or the Benito salad with heart of palm, artichokes, etc.

Entrees include fresh made soup or salade maison, and fresh vegetables. Desserts are worth trying but don't count calories. A prestigious wine list is worthy of review. The staff is accomodating and very willing to please. These are two superb restaurants by any standard.

- **HOURS: Mon. thru Sun.: 5:30 p.m.–11:00 p.m.**
  Open for lunch Phoenix only
- **CLOSING DAYS: None**
- **RESERVATIONS: Yes**
- **PARKING: Lots and valet**
- **CREDIT CARDS: All**
- **HANDICAPPED ACCESS: No difficulty in Scottsdale; two low steps at Thomas Road**
- **AVERAGE CHECK FOR TWO: $50.00**

Ayako of Tokyo

Biltmore Fashion Park
2564 E. Camelback Road — 955-7007
Phoenix — 955-0777

PHOENIX

The surroundings are authentic Nippon with a comfortable cocktail lounge, a sushi bar, and a teppanyaki dining room. However, the food is Americanized Japanese. The sushi bar, adjoining the cocktail lounge, has a great selection of fresh raw fish sushi and sashimi morsels.

It is the teppanyaki room where the chef performs his magic ringside. With twirling knives and clever wrist action the meats, vegetables and beansprouts dance and jump. You have the choice of filet mignon, steak, chicken, shrimp, scallops or lobster — either individually or in combination. Everything is sliced bite-size and appropriate for chopsticks. You order a la carte or dinner combinations, which include a tasty soup, a zippy iceberg lettuce salad, steamed rice and green tea. However, the salad is not saved by a savory dressing. The Imperial Dinner with lobster and choice of scallops or shrimp and filet mignon and N.Y. cut steak is good.

Table service by kimono-clad waitresses varies and you may have to wait until eight people have filled your teppanyaki table. The mixed drinks are so-so, but the cold Japanese beer is excellent and the hot saki authentic.

- **HOURS: Mon. thru Thurs.: 5:00 p.m.–10:00 p.m.**
  Fri. and Sat.: 5:00 p.m.–10:30 p.m.
  Sun.: 5:00 p.m.–9:30 p.m.
  Open for lunch
- **CLOSING DAYS: None**
- **RESERVATIONS: Yes**
- **PARKING: Shopping center lot**
- **CREDIT CARDS: All**
- **HANDICAPPED ACCESS: No difficulty**
- **AVERAGE CHECK FOR TWO: $40.00**

* * * *American*

The Bistro

Biltmore Financial Center
2398 E. Camelback Road
Phoenix 957-3214

PHOENIX

The pink marble floor with mahogany chairs and banquettes, plus outside patio dining, will stir memories of an up-scale Parisian bistro. It is somewhat crowded, can be noisy, but a joie de vivre and conviviality permeates the scene. This is the Left Bank transplated to Phoenix.

Although the setting is French, the a la carte bill of fare is American with only a slight nod to Europe. Thus, from an open display kitchen you can enjoy veal osso buco with grilled eggplant and white beans, grilled smoked squab with roasted garlic, potatoes and leek puree, sauteed duckling with turnips and prunes in shallots sauce, grilled marlin with red lentils, green beans and herbs. Appetizers range from smoked Norwegian salmon to caviar and foie gras. Salads range from mixed green and endive with walnut-pecan dressing to a fresh mozzarella and tomatoes, and a grilled sea scallop or grilled chicken salad. The menu is changed frequently.

The separate dessert menu includes many of the famous creations from next door Christopher's, and any selection is a fabulous climax to a super meal. The wine list is international in scope and lists many labels available by the glass. Waiter service is smart and efficient.

- **HOURS: Mon. thru Sun.: 5:00 p.m.–10:00 p.m.**
  Open for lunch
- **CLOSING DAYS: None**
- **RESERVATIONS: Yes**
- **PARKING: Lot and valet**
- **CREDIT CARDS: All**
- **HANDICAPPED: No difficulty**
- **AVERAGE CHECK FOR TWO: $55.00**

Black Angus

A total of six convenient locations in the Valley of the Sun and one in Tucson. Consult your telephone directory for addresses.

PHX – TEMPE – MESA – SCTSDL – TUCSON

This is a growing restaurant chain with a special charm and informal conviviality. It is good wholesome American cooking, nothing terribly complicated, and at the right price.

The restaurants are replicas of old ranch barns with rough wood, rafters and vaulting beams. There are comfortable, candle-lit bar-lounges with soft upholstered wall benchs and stuffed hassocks that make it very easy to hang around for more than one drink. Dining is in private, plexiglass cubicles where conversation cannot easily be overheard.

Beef is king on the menu and there is a wide choice of steaks, filet mignon and prime rib. All are quite good and satisfying. They have recently added some chicken and seafood entrees, and some of these are available in combination with beef items. You have a choice of a good soup, a mediocre iceberg lettuce salad, or a fresh made cole slaw with the meal. The fresh baked whole wheat bread is tasty. The apple tart is a good dessert.

The wine list is minimal. The table service has always been excellent and above average.

- **HOURS:** **Mon. thru Thurs.: 5:00 p.m.–10:30 p.m.**
Fri. and Sat.: 5:00 p.m.–11:30 p.m.
Sun.: 12 noon–10:00 p.m.
Open for lunch
- **CLOSING DAYS: None**
- **RESERVATIONS: Yes**
- **PARKING: Lot**
- **CREDIT CARDS: All**
- **HANDICAPPED ACCESS: Gentle ramps where needed**
- **AVERAGE CHECK FOR TWO: $26.00**

Black Bart's

2760 E. Butler Avenue
Flagstaff 779-3142

FLAGSTAFF

Enjoy the era of yesteryear with singing waiters and waitresses, a rinky tink piano, a cowboy saloon and (during the summer only) an old west dinner theatre with vaudeville and melodrama. All this plus very good vittles! It's in a barn-like eaterie with stuffed deer and buffalo heads, as well as green plants and whiffletrees hanging from rafters and beams.

The bill of fare is short and simple: six sizes and kinds of oak broiled steaks, plus ground beef and steak on a stick, deep fried shrimp, and broiled or barbecued chicken. Go for the steaks — the Rustler's Special being our favorite and the best. With your steak you get a "leaves and weeds" salad, which is only a mediocre pile of iceberg lettuce with croutons and tomatoes; a generous portion of cowboy beans in a cast iron pot (with special hot "salsa" on the side!); and good sourdough biscuits with honey butter.

It's extra for French fries or a baked potato. A rather good deep fried cinnamon ice cream is the only dessert. The grape chart is a modest wine list with reasonable prices. Table service is usually fast with energetic college students from N.A.U. making up in speed for what they lack in experience.

- **HOURS: Mon. thru Thurs.: 5:00 p.m.–9:00 p.m.**
  Fri. and Sat.: 5:00 p.m.–10:00 p.m.
- **CLOSING DAYS: None**
- **RESERVATIONS: No**
- **PARKING: Lot**
- **CREDIT CARDS: MC, V**
- **HANDICAPPED ACCESS: No difficulty**
- **AVERAGE CHECK FOR TWO: $32.00**

Bobby McGee's

8501 N. 27th Avenue, Phoenix 995-5982
1320 W. Southern, Mesa 969-4600
6900 E. Shea Blvd., Scottsdale 998-5591
6464 E. Tanque Verde Rd., Tucson 886-5551

PHOENIX – MESA – SCOTTSDALE – TUCSON

Here's a real razzle-dazzle of a place. Bring the kids — they'll love it and so will you. Some of the tables are old whiskey packing crates and some of the seats at the tables are modified old toilets. There's an old dentist chair, antique chandeliers, a pot-bellied stove, and the color schemes are out of this world. The waiters and waitresses are all dressed in costumes (there's Superman, Zorro, Heidi, Robin Hood, and many more) and they have personalities to match. The hostesses are right out of Gone With the Wind. It's thoroughly delightful.

The serve-yourself salad bar is a giant bathtub where the beef-barley, pea or lentil soups are tops, and the salad selections include mixed greens, firm cherry tomatoes, raw mushrooms, raisins and other crisp garden goodies and four or more dressings.

The steaks and three cuts of prime rib have usually been good; the beef brochette somehow misses the mark. The wild rice they serve is a little meager on the wild part, but the staff makes up for it. The French fries and baked potatoes are the best. With each meal comes a warm, delicious, round loaf of bread. The wine list is brief but covers the essentials.

- **HOURS: Sun. thru Thurs.: 5:00 p.m.–10:00 p.m.**
  Fri. and Sat.: 5:00 p.m.–11:00 p.m.
- **CLOSING DAYS: None**
- **RESERVATIONS: Yes**
- **PARKING: Lots**
- **CREDIT CARDS: All**
- **HANDICAPPED ACCESS: No difficulty**
- **AVERAGE CHECK FOR TWO: $35.00**

Italian
French

Boccata

River Center
5605 E. River Road
Tucson 577-9309

TUCSON

A new star has risen on the culinary horizon of Tucson. Orbiting on the second floor of the River Center, you enjoy fine dining with a great city view through picture windows or from a sheltered terrace.

The sophisticated menu is a talented mix of northern Italian and south French cooking. The linguini with smoked salmon and herbed goat cheese in a velvety cream sauce, and the tenderloin of pork with carmelized onions, pine nuts and raisins are both stellar creations. The calves liver sauteed with red wine and shallots, and the loin lamb chops bring no complaint. Steaks and veal have disappointed although the quality of the meat is more at fault than the kitchen.

All meals come with potato of the day or rice. Salads are a la carte but they prepare an excellent dark green salad with a nice vinaigrette and grated parmesan cheese. There is also a zingy endive salad with blue cheese and walnuts. The chocolate sin flourless chocolate cake is a must for desserts. The modest wine list has some interesting labels at fair prices. Waiters in bow ties and cafe aprons are friendly and accomodating.

- **HOURS: Sun. thru Thurs.: 5:00 p.m.–9:00 p.m.**
  Fri. and Sat.: 5:00 p.m.–10:00 p.m.
- **CLOSING DAYS: Month of Aug.** • **RESERVATIONS: Yes**
- **PARKING: Shopping center lot** • **CREDIT CARDS: MC, V**
- **HANDICAPPED ACCESS: Elevator to second floor**
- **AVERAGE CHECK FOR TWO $38.00**

* * *Continental*

Briarwood at the Park

2121 E. Highland Avenue
Phoenix 955-2060

PHOENIX

Amidst a romantic blend of rich oak paneling, beveled glass and antiques, a special dining experience awaits. A beamed ceiling with a lot of architectural angles holds brass chandeliers over two levels of sophisticated dining. Lovely floral china graces tables and booths.

The prix fixe menu, based on the entree price, includes everything from lavish appetizers, through salads, a choice of two dozen classically prepared main courses, dessert and beverage. It is a magnificent epicurean occasion. The meal begins with an appetizer tray featuring fresh shrimp steamed in beer, liver pate, smoked salmon butter, chilled ratatouille, mushrooms Dorchester and selected cheeses for spreading. This is followed by your choice of spinach salad with hot bacon dressing or a tossed green salad.

Dinner entrees include filet Wellington done in the classic manner, pepper steak au cognac, duck amaretto, chicken Rochambeau, roast pheasant and three veal dishes. Fresh vegetable of the day, saffron rice or a baked potato accompany the meal.

The extensive wine cellar offers over 150 of some of the world's finest selections at reasonable prices. To complete the repast, Briarwood serves a large tray of assorted fruit and chocolate brownies. Table service is usually first rate.

- **HOURS: Mon. thru Sun.: 5:30 p.m.—10:30 p.m.**
  Open for lunch
- **CLOSING DAYS: None**
- **RESERVATIONS: Yes**
- **PARKING: Lot and valet**
- **CREDIT CARDS: All**
- **HANDICAPPED ACCESS: No difficulty**
- **AVERAGE CHECK FOR TWO: $50.00**

Mexican
Spanish

Cafe La Tasca

The Mercado
541 E. Van Buren Street
Phoenix

340-8797

PHOENIX

This is a cutesy "South of the Border" place that promises more than it delivers. Piped in music is lively and a full service bar pours high voltage drinks. A display kitchen is open to view, and black floors and colorful walls give it a barrio, barroom appearance. Outside dining under umbrellas is pleasant.

The Mexican dishes are recipes from the central plateau and include marinated roast pork wrapped in banana leaves, and grilled chicken breasts with mole, white rice and black beans. Both are expertly cooked and given panache with touches of herbs. Among the Castilian entrees stick to the paella Valenciana for two. It is a bountiful combo of shrimp, clams, mussels, squid, scallops, etc. in a sparkling broth.

There is a special menu for hot and cold tapas, those bite-size snacks that are fried, grilled, baked, etc. and eaten with the fork or fingers with drinks. They range from morsels of fried squid, steamed mussels and garlic marinated artichokes to chorizo sausage, ham Serrano and Mexican cheeses. Some are nice and some are a bit wimpy. The flan carmel dessert is fantastico.

- **HOURS: Mon. thru Sat.: 4:00 p.m.–10:00 p.m.**
  Sun.: 11:00 a.m.–6:00 p.m.
  Open for lunch
- **CLOSING DAYS: None**
- **RESERVATIONS: Yes**
- **PARKING: Lot and street**
- **CREDIT CARDS: All**
- **HANDICAPPED ACCESS: No difficulty**
- **AVERAGE CHECK FOR TWO: $28.00**

* * *Italian*

Cafe Niko

La Camarilla
5320 E. Shea Boulevard
Scottsdale 998-1546

SCOTTSDALE

Although located in a health club, this dining room emanates a comfortable, peaceful ambience in spite of the hustle-bustle outside. Large picture windows overlook the net action on several tennis courts. Low pony walls separate a cozy all-service bar from the immaculately set tables adorned with fresh flowers.

The menu is basically Italian with a few Greek touches. The 10-item pasta list avoids commonplace spaghetti but includes an innovative and tasta spinach pasta with salmon, peas and Alfredo sauce. The perfect grilled rack of lamb with feta cheese on the side is royal fare. Likewise the saltimboca Florentine, veal Michelle and chicken Sorrentino are great. The chef also has expertise with eggplant and uses it to advantage in several dishes.

All entrees are served with a decent soup or salad, fresh steamed veggies and heavenly, warm garlic bread sticks. The dinner salad is made of boring iceburg lettuce, but on request they will use tasty romaine. The creamy Italian house dressing is exquisite. Desserts are fancy and rich. The wine list is properly diverse with a nice range and fair prices. Table service is gracious and attentive. For the price and setting Niko's is a real winner.

- **HOURS: Mon. thru Sun.: 5:00 p.m.–10:00 p.m.**
  Open for lunch
- **CLOSING DAYS: None**
- **RESERVATIONS: Yes**
- **PARKING: Lot**
- **CREDIT CARDS: All**
- **HANDICAPPED ACCESS: No difficulty**
- **AVERAGE CHECK FOR TWO: $27.00**

Cafe Terra Cotta

St. Philip's Plaza
4310 N. Campbell Avenue (River Road)
Tucson 577-8100

TUCSON

In St. Philip's Plaza, this is a culinary trend-setter that will shake and rattle boring menus in dull and unimaginative eating places. Cafe Terra Cotta is today, and it is on the cutting edge of the new American cuisine. The restaurant is bright and airy making imaginative use of color to set the scene for dining enjoyment. A small cactus is on every table and other greenery accent the room.

The innovative bill of fare never fails to excite. Try to decide among prawns stuffed with herbed goat cheese and coated with tomato coulis; grilled salmon with sour cream, tomato garlic and mint salsa; smoked pork loin with white bean chili and salsa; a mixed grill of quail, lamb chop, shrimp and chorizo with chipotle aioli; grilled lamb chops with cranberries and cassis. Desserts are fascinating: three-layer almond cake with coffee, butterscotch and chocolate glaze; almond tort with raspberry sauce; creme brulee with fresh fruit, etc. All are mouthwatering.

Pizzas are baked in a wood burning oven that imparts a special, delicate taste. The Arizona cole slaw includes avocado and jicama as well as the crisp cabbage. The raw mushroom, Jarlsberg cheese and parsley salad is another remarkable dish.

- **HOURS: Sun. thru Thurs.: 5:00 p.m.–10:00 p.m.**
  Fri. and Sat.: 5:00 p.m.–11:00 p.m.
  Open for lunch
- **CLOSING DAYS: None**
- **RESERVATIONS: Yes**
- **PARKING: Shopping center lot**
- **CREDIT CARDS: All**
- **HANDICAPPED ACCESS: No difficulty**
- **AVERAGE CHECK FOR TWO: $38.00**

Canyon Rose

Los Abrigados Resort
160 Portal Lane　　282-7673
Sedona　　282-1777

SEDONA

Nestled adjacent to Tlaquepaque is one of Sedona's newest posh resorts, and in its premier dining room you can dine grandly. A southwest tone is set with dusty rose tablecloths and Indian patterns on padded chairs. Hanging globed chandeliers, fine china and a flower and candle on tables give a touch of luxury.

The menu is not extensive, but gastronomic delights abound. The classic Caesar salad is authentic Italian, and the prime midwestern beef items from tenderloin tournedos and N.Y. strip steak to the filet mignon with bearnaise sauce are broiled to perfection. The roast rack of Colorado lamb lacks excitement and the same is true of the grilled veal scallops. Although frozen, the kitchen displays talent in the handling of the baked Atlantic salmon, Florida snapper and the seafood mixed grill. The exciting sauces make a big difference.

All entrees include potato or rice, a vegetable and a delightful dinner salad with tempting dressings. Dessert time brings an array of pastries — some premises made. The wine list is choice but a bit overpriced. Table service is polished. On Wednesday nights there is an outstanding Mexican buffet that should not be missed.

- **HOURS: Mon. thru Sun.: 5:00 p.m.–10:00 p.m.**
  Open for lunch; brunch on Sunday
- **CLOSING DAYS: None**
- **RESERVATIONS: Yes**
- **PARKING: Lot**
- **CREDIT CARDS: All**
- **HANDICAPPED ACCESS: Four steps**
- **AVERAGE CHECK FOR TWO: $45.00**

Captain's Table

Nautical Inn
1000 McCulloch Boulevard
Lake Havasu City 855-2141

LAKE HAVASU CITY

Overlooking the Colorado River and the bustling activity of a marina, this two-level dining room sets the benchmark for meals in the Lake Havasu area. There are booths and tables in a quiet ambience of green and beige. Reserve early for a window table.

The chef does not overreach and sets a nice balance between beef, veal, chicken and seafood. If you like vegetables go for the stir fried cashew chicken with abundant nuts, green peppers, broccoli, bean sprouts, and pea pods on a bed of rice with oriental sauce. The pasta part of the chicken fettucine does not pass muster. However, the lemon veal and veal Parmigiana are satisfying as are the lime broiled halibut and shrimp scampi. Locals go strong for the Mariner's Combo of lobster, king crab, shrimp and scallops. The steaks and filet mignon deserve neither praise or criticism.

Entrees include an average salad or daily soup, potato or rice, a bread loaf and butter. Creme de menthe over vanilla ice cream is the best dessert. The wine list covers the essentials, and table service is mechanical and bored. The reduced-price Sunset Dinners to 7:00 p.m. are a bargain.

- **HOURS: Sun. thru Thurs.: 5:00 p.m.–9:00 p.m.**
  Fri. and Sat.: 5:00 p.m.–10:00 p.m.
  Open for lunch
- **CLOSING DAYS: None** • **RESERVATIONS: Yes**
- **PARKING: Lot** • **CREDIT CARDS: All**
- **HANDICAPPED ACCESS: Several steps inside**
- **AVERAGE CHECK FOR TWO: $30.00**

* *

Italian

Carmelo's

El Pueblo Plaza
8140 N. Hayden Road
Scottsdale

443-3096

SCOTTSDALE

Enjoy the romance and splendor of Italy at this sophisticated eatery in one of the chic shopping centers in the McCormick Ranch area. Indirect lighting casts a pink glow over the two-room dining area of immaculate tables and upholstered chairs. There is also pleasant dining in an outdoor courtyard.

Be sure to check out the enticing antipasto and dessert display at the entrance. It sets the tone for the meal: fresh ingredients, a beautiful presentation and mouth-watering creations. With a warm loaf of delicious bread comes a ramekin of herbed olive oil with Parmesan cheese for dipping. The a la carte dinner salad is a nice mixture of raw, crisp vegetables, minimum lettuce, and a beautifully balanced walnut vinaigrette dressing. The pasta dishes are a joy to behold and taste: fettucine with crabmeat, capelli with smoked salmon, black pepper fettucine with oysters and mushrooms, etc. The chicken dishes and the grilled breast of duck will not disappoint. Fresh grilled salmon over spinach with garlic and other fresh fish dishes are royal fare.

The wine list stresses Italian and California varieties. Table service is professional. When dinner is done you know you have dined grandly.

- **HOURS: Mon. thru Sat.: 5:30 p.m.–11:00 p.m.**
  Sun.: 5:30 p.m.–9:30 p.m.
  Open for lunch
- **CLOSING DAYS: None**
- **RESERVATIONS: Yes**
- **PARKING: Lot**
- **CREDIT CARDS: All**
- **HANDICAPPED ACCESS: No difficulty**
- **AVERAGE CHECK FOR TWO: $46.00**

Casa Molina

6225 E. Speedway Boulevard
Tucson 886-5468

TUCSON

For authentic Mexican food prepared by a skilled native chef, this is the place. A Tucson landmark for over 40 years, this rustic restaurant is in an old pioneer adobe home with raftered ceilings, cement floors and thick walls. There are three dining rooms with polished wooden tables plus outside patio dining. Unique among Arizona restaurants the Casa Molina cordially invites you to inspect their kitchens.

The fascinating menu offers a complete selection of Mexican dishes using time tested Molina family recipes. There are long lists of superior tacos, enchiladas, tostadas, chimichangas, burros, etc. Or if you prefer then partake of any of 10 complete dinners, which include a choice of a bean tostada or chicken rice soup. Also, do not overlook the glorified enchilada specialty of the house, or the steak and cheese enchilada. These are both fabulous creations.

With the warm taco chips, presented on being seated, comes a terrific homemade chiletipin hot sauce that will really open your sinuses. The sangria and wines are generally standard but the tangy Margaritas are sensational. Waiter service is fast and efficient. On weekend evenings there is a lively mariachi band.

- **HOURS: Mon. thru Sun.: 4:00 p.m.–10:00 p.m.**
  Open for lunch
- **CLOSING DAYS: None**
- **RESERVATIONS: Yes**
- **PARKING: Lot**
- **CREDIT CARDS: All**
- **HANDICAPPED ACCESS: No difficulty**
- **AVERAGE CHECK FOR TWO: $23.00**

* * *Continental*

Chaparral Room

Camelback Inn
5402 E. Lincoln Drive — 948-1700
Scottsdale — 948-6644

SCOTTSDALE

With picturesque Camelback Mountain as a backdrop, here is distinctive dining in a southwest setting at one of the Valley's most elegant resorts. The atmosphere is soft, warm and comfortable.

The menu keeps changing and improving. The appetizers (escargots, coquille St. Jacques), the lobster bisque with cream and caviar, and the special salads (spinach and Caesar, and salad Antoinette with pinenuts) continue to soar to new heights.

The sauteed veal loin with crabmeat, lobster and shrimp, and the roasted rack of lamb are sensational and are highly recommended. The chicken and fish dishes are impeccable. The roast duckling with a kiwi-fresh ginger sauce is perfect, as is the beef Wellington and the roast loin of lamb with spinach and endive. The fresh-baked dinner rolls are not to be missed.

The dessert pastries and other sweets are homemade and worth loosening your belt for. The chocolate souffle is grand, and the dinner coffee is served with separate whipped cream, cinnamon sticks, chocolate chips and licorice! The wine list has depth and range, and represents obvious care; table service is competent and professional without being stiff.

- **HOURS: Sun. thru Thurs.: 6:00 p.m.–10:00 p.m.**
  Fri. and Sat.: 6:00 p.m.–11:00 p.m.
- **CLOSING DAYS: None**
- **RESERVATIONS: Yes**
- **PARKING: Lot and valet**
- **CREDIT CARDS: All**
- **HANDICAPPED ACCESS: Several small steps at both dining room and hotel entrances**
- **AVERAGE CHECK FOR TWO: $65.00**

* * * *Continental*

Charles

6400 E. El Dorado Circle (Wilmot)
Tucson 296-7173

TUCSON

A majestic driveway lined with 60-foot cypress trees leads to a cobblestone courtyard and on to a stately English manor house — the Charles. The interior, in keeping with the exterior, is warm and elegant. The large arched windows, rich multicolored carpet, white tablecloths, flowers and pewter serving pieces set the stage for luxurious dining in a setting of tranquility.

The epicurean experience begins with some extravagant a la carte appetizers. Then follow daily fresh soups and garden crisp salads that taste as good as they look. The chef's culinary wizardry is deftly demonstrated in the entrees, be it veal, beef, poultry, fish or seafood. Veal Charles with lobster medallions and bearnaise sauce is the acclaimed specialty of the house and is nirvana. On the same celestial level are shrimp and scallops a la Greque with feta cheese, the tender steak Diane and the chef's unique creations of the day. The beef Wellington is sensational and the zesty pepper steak flambe is prepared tableside with a flair.

Meals include choice of soup or salad, vegetable, potato and hot breads. Desserts are delectable and include pastries, chocolate mousse, flamed desserts and a souffle du jour not to be missed. Service is polished without being stuffy and the wine list is superior.

- **HOURS: Mon. thru Sun.: 6:00 p.m.–9:00 p.m.**
  Open for lunch
- **CLOSING DAYS: Month of July**
- **RESERVATIONS: Yes**
- **PARKING: Lot and valet**
- **CREDIT CARDS: All**
- **HANDICAPPED ACCESS: Three steps at entrance**
- **AVERAGE CHECK FOR TWO: $55.00**

Charlie Clark's (Gibson's)

Highway #260
Pinetop 367-4900

PINETOP – LAKESIDE

Pleasant and enjoyable dining in two large, connected rooms that retain a frontier ambience with a grizzly bear hide on the wall, Indian kachina dolls, electrified kerosine lantern chandeliers, a pot bellied stove and lots of woodwork. It's no surprise that Charlie Clark's been packin' em in since 1938.

The fare is no challenge to the imagination, just hearty good food with good service at reasonable prices. The steaks and chops are served "Western Style" with sauteed bell peppers, onions, sliced mushrooms and salsa. Depending on the cuts and types, tasty steaks come in 6-, 8-, 10-, and 12-oz. sizes. Many locals swear the chicken fried steak is the best in Arizona, and the tender filet mignon has never brought a complaint. The chef has a special touch with the seafood items, even though most are frozen.

Along with your steak you get a trip to the best and most attractive soup and salad bar in Navajo County, a choice of potato, rice or vegetable, and nice hot bread. There is a long list of desserts, but regrettably none are products of the house chef. The wine list complements the steaks and prices are not out of line. Waitress service is casual but they get the job done.

- **HOURS: Mon., Wed. thru Sat.: 5:00 p.m.–10:00 p.m.**
  Sun.: 5:00 p.m.–9:00 p.m.
  Open for lunch
- **CLOSING DAYS: Tues.**
- **RESERVATIONS: Yes**
- **PARKING: Lot**
- **CREDIT CARDS: All**
- **HANDICAPPED ACCESS: No difficulty**
- **AVERAGE CHECK FOR TWO: $35.00**

Charlie's

Crescent Hotel
2620 W. Dunlap Avenue
Phoenix 943-8200

PHOENIX

On two levels guests can savor the culinary delights of an inspired master chef in a rich atmosphere colored with hues of mauve and plum accented with polished marble and stone. A European setting of elegant simplicity is achieved.

The extensive uncluttered menu is choice and forthright. Everything is a la carte and a salad is not included with the price of the entree. Variety is nicely balanced with beef, veal, lamb and poultry dishes harmonizing with a simple vegetable plate. More simple fare with a magic touch includes broiled Norwegian salmon with sauce bearnaise, orange roughy Chino, broiled lamb chops with jalapeno jelly, medallions of veal with morel mushrooms in cream, filet mignon and N.Y. strip steak. If you are a lamb fancier go for the roast rack of lamb.

There are almost as many appetizers, soups and salads as entrees — and some are certain to tingle your tastebuds. A selection of yummy pastries, all baked on the premises, is presented for dessert. The chocolate tower is an award winner. If you have never tried it the creme brulee with fresh raspberries and toasted almonds is a masterpiece here. The wine list is above reproach. Table service is usually attentive and solicitous.

- **HOURS: Mon. thru Sun.: 6:00 p.m.–10:30 p.m.**
  Open for breakfast, lunch; brunch on Sun.
- **CLOSING DAYS: None** • **RESERVATIONS: Yes**
- **PARKING: Lot, valet and garage** • **CREDIT CARDS: All**
- **HANDICAPPED ACCESS: No difficulty**
- **AVERAGE CHECK FOR TWO: $52.00**

Chez Song

Ranch Center
9030 E. Via Linda (Pima)
Scottsdale 860-1509

SCOTTSDALE

Just east of Pima Road on McCormick Ranch is one of the most attractive Chinese restaurants in Arizona. A predominance of shades of lavender, red and aqua, plus green plants, Chinese art on the walls and a dramatic high ceiling make this place a standout.

They specialize in Mandarin, Hunan and Szechuan cuisine with the spicy hot dishes printed in the menu in red. After several visits with friends the following stand out: the curry shrimp; shrimp, scallops and chicken on a golden rice crust; Kung Pao two, shrimp and chicken with peanuts; lemon chicken; house special chicken; ginger beef; Mongolian and Genghis Khan beef. We have been less happy with the heavy crepes for the mu-shu shrimp, pork and chicken, the overcooked duck dishes and the syrupy sweet-sour sauce. However, the pot stickers are excellent and among the best we have eaten.

There are the usual complete dinners from $8.95 to $13.95 per person — minimum service two. Steamed rice and hot tea with all dishes are standard along with the finale fortune cookies and their bland messages. Warning: avoid the tight, cramped booths — ask for a table and spare your legs and back.

- **HOURS: Mon. thru Sat.: 4:30 p.m.–10:00 p.m.**
Sun.: 4:30 p.m.–9:30 p.m.
Open for lunch including Sat.
- **CLOSING DAYS: None**
- **RESERVATIONS: Yes**
- **PARKING: Lot**
- **CREDIT CARDS: All**
- **HANDICAPPED ACCESS: No difficulty**
- **AVERAGE CHECK FOR TWO: $23.00**

Chianti Trattoria

3939 E. Camelback Road
Phoenix 957-9840

PHOENIX

This is Tomaso's attempt to bring modest prices to good food in a bistro environment of inviting cordiality. By and large the idea works. Once inside Chianti you are in Rome — not the Via Veneto mind you, but certainly the stradas to the side. Large photos of world celebrities cover the walls.

The bill of fare is small but ranges from pizza to complete dinners of shrimp, veal and chicken. There is offered an excellent cold antipasto, three salads, 10 pasta dishes, seven specialty entrees plus three seafood and a couple of cheese and tomato pizzas. The chicken or shrimp marinara on a bed of linguini is generous and taste perfect. Likewise the chicken cacciatore and Siciliana are everything hoped for. The chicken, veal and eggplant Parmigiana are all tender dreams. None of the above will disappoint. We have also been pleased with other eggplant dishes and fresh fish specials. The calamari fra-diavolo and the seafood Portafino are super.

A side order of al dente pasta comes with all entrees. An average tossed green salad is extra. Cheesecakes are the best desserts. The modest priced wine list supports the meals. Table service is brisk and attentive.

- **HOURS: Mon. thru Sat.: 5:00 p.m.–10:30 p.m.**
  Sun.: 4:00 p.m.–10.00 p.m.
  Open for lunch
- **CLOSING DAYS: None**
- **RESERVATIONS: Yes**
- **PARKING: Shopping center lot**
- **CREDIT CARDS: All**
- **HANDICAPPED ACCESS: No difficulty**
- **AVERAGE CHECK FOR TWO: $28.00**

China Gate

7820 E. McDowell Rd., Scottsdale	946-0720
1815 E. Camelback Rd., Phoenix	264-2600
3033 W. Peoria Ave., Phoenix	944-1982
2050 W. Guadalupe Road, Mesa	897-0607

SCOTTSDALE – PHOENIX – MESA

Bored with the same old ubiquitous Chinese dishes served from San Francisco to New York? Looking for new gustatory thrills? Well, China Gate is the place for you. Yes, China Gate serves moo goo gai pan, cashew and lemon chicken, sweet and sour shrimp, Peking duck, chow mein, etc., but you can also get jellyfish, some beautiful crab dishes, mushrooms with snails, seaweed soup, and much more. There are several lamb entrees, and if you like it hot there is volcano beef! Deep fried mushrooms old hat? Try China Gate's dancing mushrooms sauteed with the chef's special aromatic sauce.

The 11-page menu, which is the most attractive and enchanting in the Valley, also boosts the Royal Dynasty Selections. These are a dollar or two higher priced than other dishes, but can you resist crab and chicken dishes with avocado, beef l'orange, etc.

The bill of fare proudly states that no MSG (monosodium glutamate) food enhancer is used in food preparation. There is also a lively, educational one-page description of the various cuisines of China. Decor is rather subdued with little more than green plants and piped-in Chinese music. An exotic drink menu rivals Trader Vic's.

- **HOURS:** **Sun. thru Thurs.: 5:00 p.m.–10:00 p.m.**
  Fri. and Sat.: 5:00 p.m.–11:00 p.m.
  Open for lunch
- **CLOSING DAYS: None**
- **RESERVATIONS: Yes**
- **PARKING: Lot**
- **CREDIT CARDS: All**
- **HANDICAPPED ACCESS: No difficulty**
- **AVERAGE CHECK FOR TWO: $22.00**

American

Chops

1371 N. Alma School Road
Chandler

899-6735

CHANDLER

This is another slick restaurant of the "Big Four" — the popular chain that has given us Oscar Taylor's, American Grill, Steamers, etc. They generally do a good job and Chops is no exception. The menu is sufficiently diverse but not overreaching, the food is good but not great, the table service is swift but not particularly professional, and the prices are reasonable although not bargains.

You dine in booths and banquettes in a multi-room complex that can be noisy. Fast moving waitresses recite fresh fish specials and we recommend you concentrate your attention here, as well as among the steak items and the mesquite broiled, center cut pork chops with a honey barbeque sauce. The prime rib, veal and chicken dishes do not thrill.

Dinners come with a "table salad bar" consisting of a bowl of disappointing iceberg lettuce with cucumber and tomato slices in a nice vinaigrette dressing. You add from a "Lazy Susan" bacon bits, cheeses, chives and shrimp. Except for the white lettuce the salad could be a standout. The au gratin-sour cream house potato is excellent, as is the fresh baked, sourdough bread loaf. "Early Bird" dinner specials from 4:00 to 6:30 p.m. Sunday thru Thursday are nice money savers.

- **HOURS:** **Sun. thru Thurs.: 4:00 p.m.–10:00 p.m.**
Fri. and Sat.: 4:00 p.m.–11:00 p.m.
Open for lunch
- **CLOSING DAYS: None**
- **RESERVATIONS: Yes**
- **PARKING: Lot**
- **CREDIT CARDS: All**
- **HANDICAPPED ACCESS: No difficulty**
- **AVERAGE CHECK FOR TWO: $29.00**

* * *American*

Christmas Tree

Broken Arrow Lodge
Woodland Lake Road
Lakeside 367-3107

PINETOP – LAKESIDE

Here is an old farmhouse at Christmastime with a colorful lighted tree in front, wreaths and holiday decorations on walls, red tablecloths and green accents. It's very festive and cheerful. Dining is in small, cozy rooms with slightly uncomfortable chairs. There is also an enclosed outdoor patio that is charming and relaxing with garden furniture and a fireplace.

The menu is basic and is not adventuresome. However, good food can be had. Locals swear by the roast chicken and dumplings, and barbecued pork ribs with cinnamon apples. We found the ample beef Stroganoff, with rice or noodles, to be superior, and we thoroughly enjoyed the two double lamb chops (pink but not red) and the succulent roast duckling with honey almond sauce — meaty, juicy and tasty. The baked shrimp and scallops lack punch but the N.Y. steak is everything hoped for.

All entrees receive a pickled beet appetizer, choice of soup or mixed green salad (the creamy bacon house dressing is great), potatoes au gratin, fresh veggies and homemade cinnamon rolls. During winter months there is a salad bar. Desserts have improved. The wine list is modest and covers the basics at fair prices.

- **HOURS: Wed. thru Sun.: 5:00 p.m.–9:00 p.m.**
- **CLOSING DAYS: Mon. and Tues.**
- **RESERVATIONS: Yes** • **CREDIT CARDS: MC, V**
- **PARKING: Lot**
- **HANDICAPPED ACCESS: No difficulty**
- **AVERAGE CHECK FOR TWO: $35.00**

* * *

French

Christopher's

Biltmore Financial Center
2398 E. Camelback Road
Phoenix

957-3214

This glittering temple of gastronomy with soft lighting, mahogany wood and a visible wine cellar sets the standard for fine dining on the Camelback Corridor. There are only 14 tables set with fine china, sparkling crystal and shining silverware. An ever-changing eclectic menu combines the freshness of nouvelle cuisine with the luxury of traditional.

In addition to a la carte selections, two complete dinners are offered, one of six courses for $60 ($85 with wines) and the other of eight courses for $75 ($110 with wines). It goes without saying that both dinners are royal fare that would do Escoffier proud. If you choose the a la carte route, then enjoy such riches as veal sweetbreads on a bed of sauteed leeks with truffle sauce, roast duck breast slices in a sauce of peppercorns and dates, rack of lamb with garlic sauce, Dover sole presented three ways, medallions of veal with tarragon and wild leek sauce. The choices go on. . . .

The salad and dessert presentations are incredible. The impeccable wine list accents French vineyards but is international in depth and scope. Smooth table service by formally dressed waiters is professional and caring. Soft background music is perfect. At meal's end you know you have dined grandly.

- **HOURS: Tues. thru Sun.: 6:00 p.m.–10:00 p.m.**
- **CLOSING DAYS: Mon.**
- **RESERVATIONS: Yes**
- **PARKING: Lot and valet**
- **CREDIT CARDS: All**
- **HANDICAPPED ACCESS: No difficulty**
- **AVERAGE CHECK FOR TWO: $120.00**

* * *Italian*

Christo's

6327 N. 7th Street (Maryland)
Phoenix 264-1784

PHOENIX

Glass blocks form pony wall partitions breaking up the spatial monotony of a lovely dining room. Table settings are crisp and immaculate with white over pink tablecloths, sparkling silverware and stemware, and a sprig of fresh flowers.

The easy to read menu lists many old Northern Italian favorites. There are five poultry items with a breast of chicken artfully mixed with mushrooms, bell peppers and tomatoes, called chicken zingarella, that seems a highlight. Of six veal dishes do not overlook the veal Christo consisting of medallions of tender veal with a blanket of crabmeat, chopped clams, bay shrimp and mushrooms in a cream sauce.

Gratefully there are only eight pasta dishes. However, any of the three fettucines will satisfy the most discriminating Roman. If you seek something a little more exotic try the rich and sinful Pasta Maison: spaghetti or fettucine with sweet butter, garlic, herbs and grated cheese, and then anointed with yoghurt and chopped parsley. If you like seafood, then go for the Pasta Fantasia: scallops, bay shrimp and pieces of calamari in a red meatless marinara sauce.

Other than chocolate covered strawberries desserts are standard Italiano. The wine list stresses Italian vineyards and prices are fair. Table service is satisfactory.

- **HOURS: Mon. thru Sun.: 5:30 p.m.–10:00 p.m.**
- **CLOSING DAYS: None**
- **RESERVATIONS: Yes**
- **PARKING: Lots**
- **CREDIT CARDS: All**
- **HANDICAPPED ACCESS: No difficulty**
- **AVERAGE CHECK FOR TWO: $38.00**

Chubb's

6522 N. 16th Street (Maryland)
Phoenix 279-3459

PHOENIX

No haute cuisine by any standard; simply some of the best cooking in town — and consistently so. The tone is old fashioned masculine with dark wood paneling and columns, pseudo cut-glass, globed chandeliers, overhead fans with booths, tables and captain's chairs. It will remind you of a cloistered, but noisy, eastern men's club circa 1925.

Prime rib and steak are staples here. The prime rib is always juicy, tasty, a top piece of beef, and above average for the Valley. It is available in two cuts (extra and half) and for a modest price two people can share an order. This added tariff is for the salad, potatoes, bread, etc. The conventional list of steaks seem acceptably good. As an afterthought they have broiled seabass, salmon and a nice moist roast chicken.

Dinners include a choice of daily soup or lettuce salad with raw mushrooms and alfalfa sprouts, and a choice of a baked potato, steak fries or rice pilaf. The house dressing for the salad is a dull 1000 Island or creamy French. Sour dough and pumpernickel breads are warm and good.

Desserts are mediocre; the wine list offers little of interest. Table service is erratic, but for the price it is unimportant.

- **HOURS: Sun. thru Thurs.: 4:30 p.m.–10:00 p.m.**
  Fri. and Sat.: 4:30 p.m.–12 midnight
  Open for lunch
- **CLOSING DAYS: None**
- **RESERVATIONS: No**
- **PARKING: Shopping center lot**
- **CREDIT CARDS: All**
- **HANDICAPPED ACCESS: No difficulty**
- **AVERAGE CHECK FOR TWO: $30.00**

Compass

Hyatt Regency Hotel
2nd Street and Adams 257-1110
Phoenix 252-1234

PHOENIX

Arizona's only rooftop revolving restaurant with a view that goes on forever. The points of the compass are all marked on the wall, and plaques tell you that Los Angeles, Denver, Salt Lake City, etc. are so many miles in this direction. It's kind of fun and exciting.

We have enjoyed the roasted herb chicken with jalapeno cheese and proscuitto in a garlic cream, and the scallops Gallette with cucumbers, mushrooms and a smooth crayfish mousse. There are combinations of prime rib and lobster tail or roasted herb chicken. There is often an off-menu specialty of the day that is usually good.

The cream of roasted eggplant soup is a pleasant change from the hum-drum, and the chilled avocado soup has real class. Salads are extra, but the Caesar, spinach and American garden are all first rate. The warm rosemary-olive bread with honey butter is to die for.

A dessert tray of pastries and fresh fruits is presented by the waitress at meals' end. The wine list is modest and prices are reasonable. The waitress service is competent.

- **HOURS: Mon. thru Sun.: 5:30 p.m.–10:00 p.m.**
  Open for lunch; brunch on Sunday
- **CLOSING DAYS: None.** • **RESERVATIONS: Yes**
- **PARKING: Validated parking in nearby garage**
- **CREDIT CARDS: All**
- **HANDICAPPED ACCESS: No difficulty. Use elevators.**
- **AVERAGE CHECK FOR TWO: $55.00**

Copper Room

Valley View Restaurant
Arnold and Main Streets
Camp Verde 567-3592

CAMP VERDE

Weather permitting, this popular spot welcomes you with a cheery fire, friendly waitresses and prompt service. Tables by picture windows overlook the Verde Valley, so try to arrive before dark and be sure to reserve in advance. The sunken bar makes a private spot to enjoy your favorite liquid refreshments.

The specialty of the house is the small filet mignon platter — two tender filets surrounded by four or five very fresh vegetables, and ringed with crispy Duchess mashed potatoes. A bargain it is at $11.25. For the light eater a single filet is available for $9.95.

All entrees include a relish tray and homemade soup or an undistinguished salad with a choice of dressings. There are chicken, veal and pork entrees as well as Guaymas shrimp, Long Island scallops or Idaho trout from $7.25 to $10.75. For the light eater try the steak sandwich or chef's salad. The Alaskan king crab legs with drawn butter for $14.95 is a special treat. The desserts are standard with the homemade cream and fruit pies being the best.

The prices are excellent and daily dinner specials are often a real bargain. If you are a stranger when you arrive, you will not be when you leave!

- **HOURS: Mon. thru Sun.: 5:00 p.m.–9:00 p.m.**
  Open for breakfast and lunch
- **CLOSING DAYS: None**
- **PARKING: Lot**
- **RESERVATIONS: Yes**
- **CREDIT CARDS: MC, V**
- **HANDICAPPED ACCESS: One small step at entrance**
- **AVERAGE CHECK FOR TWO: $25.00**

Cork 'N Cleaver

5101 N. 44th Street (Camelback)
Phoenix 952-0585

PHOENIX

A small bistro with a pleasant ambience and intimate atmosphere for your dining pleasure. Quiet piped-in music, candles and soft lights enhance colorful De Grazia reproductions and pioneer artifacts on the walls.

The Cork 'N Cleaver boasts of serving the best steaks you'll ever eat. They range from top sirloin and New York cut, down to marinated teriyaki sirloin and beef kabob. The prime rib is usually quite good and is available in two cuts. The anti-beef crowd will enjoy the scallops and marinated Hawaiian chicken. There are the usual combinations: steak and lobster, etc. Off-menu fish items are usually good.

With all entrees you get a trip to an above average 25-item salad bar. There are two kinds of lettuce, spinach leaves, tomatoes, onions, cucumbers, grated cheese, fruits, macaroni and potato salads, olives — even caviar and jelly beans! Don't miss the cream of broccoli soup — it's divine. There are side orders of sauteed mushrooms, artichokes, and baked potatoes.

The mud pie, with either mocha or mint chocolate chip ice cream, is not to be missed. The wine list is adequate and covers the essentials; table service is pleasant and professional by eager college types.

- **HOURS: Mon. thru Sun.: 5:30 p.m.–10:00 p.m.**
  Open for lunch
- **CLOSING DAYS: None**
- **RESERVATIONS: Up to 25% of capacity**
- **PARKING: Lot** • **CREDIT CARDS: All**
- **HANDICAPPED ACCESS: No difficulty**
- **AVERAGE CHECK FOR TWO: $36.00**

* * *Continental*

Cottage Place

126 W. Cottage Avenue
Flagstaff 774-8431

FLAGSTAFF

On a narrow residential side street that has seen better days is an old home, reeking of 1920's nostalgia, that has been converted to a charming small restaurant by a master chef. This is a hidden gem that has too long been a secret of the locals.

The menu is an epicure's dream and most dishes are deserving of an award. An acceptable pate with crudites is presented on being seated. Your meal includes a freshmade soup of the evening, a tossed green salad and a choice of four magical dressings, potato du jour or rice pilaf and a fresh garden vegetable.

The mushroom savories (stuffed with sausage and cheese) and the escargots en cocotte are very worthy appetizers. The Hungarian porkolt, rich cubes of boneless pork loin simmered with onions, green peppers and tomatoes and seasoned with sweet paprika and served on buttered noodles, is a superb entree. Likewise the Bavarian chicken embellished with sour cream is memorable. There is also leg of lamb, prime rib, veal cordon bleu, shrimp scampi, roast duck l'orange and a couple of off menu items. None have ever disappointed.

The desserts at $3.50 each are fabulous. The wine list is quite extensive. The after dinner coffee list deserves consideration. Table service is quiet and efficient.

- **HOURS: Tues. thru Sun.: 5:00 p.m.–10:00 p.m.**
- **CLOSING DAYS: Mon.**
- **RESERVATIONS: Yes**
- **PARKING: Street and small lot**
- **CREDIT CARDS: All**
- **HANDICAPPED ACCESS: Steps in front**
- **AVERAGE CHECK FOR TWO: $36.00**

Crozier's (Gibson's)

Highway #260
Pinetop 367-5555

PINETOP – LAKESIDE

On the main road in Pinetop, this rustic, grey-painted restaurant has long been a popular spot for locals and tourists alike. A small bar plus two medium sized dining rooms (tables and chairs only — no booths or banquettes) are warm and inviting. New owners have taken over but the chef remained.

The extensive menu has something for everyone from steaks, chicken and veal to seafood, pork, pheasant, quail and rack of lamb. Portions are ample and no one will go away hungry. We suggest the diner choose from the medallions of beef bearnaise; medallions of veal Oscar, Parmigiana, piccata or bearnaise; roast duckling or (and best of all) the fresh trout Barnie. This last is a stream trout, sauteed, and served with asparagus, pieces of king crab, coated with Hollandaise sauce with toasted almonds on a bed of mixed rice. It is a beautiful culinary creation that deserves high praise. Other frozen fish dishes fail to excite.

All entrees come with an invitation to a modest soup-salad bar with standard items. The homemade breadloaf fails to excite. Dessert choices are undistinguished. Table service is uneven. The organ music is pleasant. Early Bird specials from 5 to 7 p.m. Sun. thru Fri. are a real bargain.

- **HOURS: Sun., Tues. thru Thurs.: 5:00 p.m.–9:30 p.m.**
  Fri. and Sat.: 5:00 p.m.–10:00 p.m.
- **CLOSING DAYS: Mon.**
- **RESERVATIONS: Yes**
- **PARKING: Lot**
- **CREDIT CARDS: All**
- **HANDICAPPED ACCESS: Ramps where needed**
- **AVERAGE CHECK FOR TWO: $32.00**

* *Int'l.*

Culinary Arts Dining

Student Center Building
Scottsdale Community College
9000 E. Chaparral Road
Scottsdale 423-6284

SCOTTSDALE

This is a real find. You taste-test the exciting cuisine of chefs-in-training at the local Culinary Arts School. The entrance is a red awning marquee near the campus parking lot. Students prepare and serve the food, and at meals' end you grade the dinner on taste, appearance, service, etc. on a report card. The rose colored dining room is windowless, but spacious and warm with indirect lighting and comfortable seating.

The menu offers splendid five-course dinners (plus beverage) for only $15. Beer and non-alcoholic wine are available for an additional $2 and $2.25. There are nine distinct menus, rotated weekly, that offer a wide selection of exciting food. You get to choose from four appetizers (salmon pate, lobster sausage in filo, asparagus souffle with walnut sauce, etc.) two soups (borscht, Vichyssoise, gazpacho, etc.) five entrees (rack of pork with ginger lime sauce, candied duck with yam puree, Singapore peacock beef, shrimp and scallops Sambuco, lamb medallions, etc.) and five desserts (chocolate truffle cake, strawberry Napoleon, Savannah banana pie, praline pecan cheesecake, fruit tarts, etc.) In total, a great experience.

- **HOURS: Wed. thru Fri.: 5:00 p.m.–10:00 p.m.**
- **CLOSING DAYS: Sat. thru Tues., and May thru Aug.**
- **RESERVATIONS: Required**
- **PARKING: Campus lot** • **CREDIT CARDS: MC, V**
- **HANDICAPPED ACCESS: No difficulty**
- **AVERAGE CHECK FOR TWO: $30.00**

Daa's Thai Room

7419 E. Indian Plaza
Scottsdale 941-9015

SCOTTSDALE

One block south of Camelback Road, this special exotic place serves exciting royal fare in a spartan atmosphere. The elegance is in what comes to the table; the surroundings are comfortably practical. The two connecting dining rooms (one is nonsmoking) have beamed ceilings, tables and chairs — no booths or banquettes.

The intriguing multi-page menu with all the fascinating dishes will require time for picking and choosing. However, good explicit translations describe the fish, fowl, beef, pork, salads, soups and vegetarian productions. And exciting they are! The neua satay skewers of marinated beef in Thai spices with cucumber and peanut sauces is savory excitement. You should also like the spicy shrimp stir-fried with ginger, onions, mushrooms and chilis; and the beef simmered with coconut milk, curry, chili and mint. For milder palates try the various stir-fried pork, chicken and beef dishes with cucumber, bell peppers, pineapple, water chestnuts, etc. Vegetarians will enjoy various stir-fried vegetables with rice or noodles in special sauces. All dishes are seasoned to your taste; are served with steamed rice.

Desserts are limited to several icy coconut ice creams and a coconut custard topped with pumpkin pieces. Table service is adequate.

- **HOURS: Sun. thru Thurs.: 5:00 p.m.–10:00 p.m.**
  Fri. and Sat.: 5:00 p.m.–11:00 p.m.
  Open for lunch
- **CLOSING DAYS: None**
- **RESERVATIONS: Yes**
- **PARKING: Street**
- **CREDIT CARDS: MC, V**
- **HANDICAPPED ACCESS: No difficulty**
- **AVERAGE CHECK FOR TWO: $24.00**

* * * *Italian*
French

Daniel's

Plaza Palomino
2930 N. Swan Road (Fort Lowell)
Tucson 742-3200

Here is dignified dining in three adjoining rooms on the second floor of a building in the Plaza Palomino. In a suave peach colored ambience of sophisticated comfort you can enjoy classic Italian cuisine with a few regional French diversions. The tables are beautifully set and the fine, gold-rimmed china is impressively monogramed.

In addition to the traditional dishes that nourished Roman emperors, the chef has shown some culinary initiative with his impressive roast duck with peas and Madeira wine sauce, and fruitti di mare: various seafood items in a zesty lime sauce tossed with vermicelli noodles. We also highly recommend the breaded veal chop stuffed with prosciutto ham and cheese, and shrimp sauteed with vegetables and enhanced with bearnaise sauce. Mercifully there is no long pasta list.

Dinner entrees include a good, daily fresh soup, an above average dinner salad with raw mushrooms and grated Parmesan cheese, fresh steamed vegetables, potato or pasta of the day, and good Italian bread with sweet butter. Desserts are limited but the carrot and amaretto cakes deserve blue ribbons. A comprehensive and reasonably priced, multi-page wine list has a nice range of Italian vintages. Table service is winning.

- **HOURS: Sun. thru Thurs.: 4:00 p.m.–9:00 p.m.**
  Fri. and Sat.: 4:00 p.m.–10:00 p.m.
- **CLOSING DAYS: None** • **RESERVATIONS: Yes**
- **PARKING: Lot** • **CREDIT CARDS: All**
- **HANDICAPPED ACCESS: Elevator to second floor**
- **AVERAGE CHECK FOR TWO: $38.00**

Don & Charlie's

7501 E. Camelback Road
Scottsdale 990-0900

SCOTTSDALE

A Chicago transplant and a name change, this is one of those dining adventures in which the total experience transcends the component parts: the food is not wonderful, but it's hearty and enjoyable. The ribs and steaks here are simple and good, if never great; the prices are reasonable, if not exactly low; the wood paneled surroundings are comfortable; the service is efficient, friendly and unpretentious.

Pork ribs are the core attraction. They come as back ribs, spare ribs, short ribs and combinations with barbecued chicken. The barbecue sauce leaves no particular impression. They have a fine "cheesy" chicken, a large breast with Mornay sauce and fresh mozzarella. The generous iceberg lettuce salad is saved with an imaginative anchovy, sour cream dressing. With each entree you also get a choice of a baked potato, double baked, French fries or potato au gratin. The potatoes au gratin are good — the others very humdrum.

The dinner rye bread is now great. The desserts are wondrous and include a good strawberry shortcake, flourless chocolate cake, a tangy key lime pie, New York cheesecake, ice cream, brandy ice and a gold brick sundae (chocolate sauce with pecans over ice cream). The wine list is nondescript.

- **HOURS: Sun. thru Thurs.: 5:00 p.m.–10:00 p.m.**
  Fri. and Sat.: 5:00 p.m.–10:30 p.m.
- **CLOSING DAYS: None**
- **RESERVATIONS: Yes**
- **PARKING: Lot and street**
- **CREDIT CARDS: All**
- **HANDICAPPED ACCESS: No difficulty**
- **AVERAGE CHECK FOR TWO: $36.00**

Eat Your Heart Out

350 Jordan Road (Apple)
Sedona 282-1471

SEDONA

Welcome to a crisply casual, informal place where the preparation of food is an art. At lunchtime it is a self-serving, buffet-cafeteria offering sandwiches and salads. At night a magic transformation takes place. Now you have waitress service, soft lights and live music. There is both inside and outside dining. Green plants and original artwork on pink walls add a touch of sophistication.

The menu is short and sweet — only 13 items. Soup and salad choices are announced by the waitress. If you are a garlic lover, go for the chicken baked with roasted garlic, mushrooms, rose wine and bay leaves. There is also pasta primavera with a light northern Italian tomato sauce rather than the higher calorie cream sauce. The red meat eaters can enjoy tasty prime rib, lamb chops and sirloin steak. Baked king salmon with coconut, cilantro and jalapeno sauce is a fascinating change and highly recommended. So is the rainbow trout with fresh basil and raspberries.

All dinners are served with soup or salad, premises-made rolls, seasonal garden vegetables, rice pilaf or stuffed potatoes. The dessert tray is overwhelming. Table service is good. A limited but attractive wine list covers the basics.

- **HOURS: Mon. thru Sat.: 5:00 p.m.–9:00 p.m.**
  Open for lunch seven days
- **CLOSING DAYS: Sun. dinner**
- **RESERVATIONS: No**
- **PARKING: Lot and street**
- **CREDIT CARDS: MC, V**
- **HANDICAPPED ACCESS: No difficulty**
- **AVERAGE CHECK FOR TWO: $30.00**

Eddie Chan's

12601 Paradise Vlge. Pkwy., Phoenix 996-9733
9699 N. Hayden Rd., Scottsdale 998-8188

PHOENIX – SCOTTSDALE

Featuring Mandarin, Hunan, Szechuan and Cantonese cuisine, this is fine dining in popular, modestly upscale dining rooms. Oriental art and calligraphy provide the Far East ambience. The Phoenix location is known as **Eddie Chan's Too.**

For a Chinese restaurant the menu is limited — meaning less than 100 dishes being offered. But that's a plus. On our visits we are always attracted to the chef's specials, which for the most part, are distinctive and great. The chef has a special touch with black pepper and uses it in sizzling black pepper beef, chicken and lobster — and all are good. There is a long list of shrimp dishes with the Mandarin shrimp, lemon shrimp and shrimp Kung Pau being notable. If pork is your thing, try the neat Nanking spicy pork and Triple Stars: a combination of fried shrimp, pork and chicken in a special sauce.

If you are hungry, a very affordable luxury meal for two or more is the Dynasty Dinner at $12.25 per person. You receive won ton soup, mu shi pork, Szechuan prawns, sweet and sour chicken, Mongolian beef, special fried rice, fortune cookies and tea. It will not disappoint.

The wine list is unexciting. Table service is fast and efficient with swift moving waiters and waitresses ever eager to please.

- **HOURS: Sun. thru Sat.: 4:30 p.m.–10:00 p.m.**
Open for lunch including Sat.
- **CLOSING DAYS: None** • **RESERVATIONS: Yes**
- **PARKING: Shopping center lots** • **CREDIT CARDS: All**
- **HANDICAPPED ACCESS: No difficulty**
- **AVERAGE CHECK FOR TWO: $23.00**

8700 Restaurant

8700 E. Pinnacle Peak Road (Pima Road)
Scottsdale 994-8700

SCOTTSDALE

At the heart of the new Citadel business complex is the austerely beautiful 8700 restaurant. Reminiscent of the architecture of Santa Fe, the prestigious dining rooms have fireplaces, contemporary artworks and antique furniture. The up-beat kitchen combines an elegance in preparation and presentation with fresh southwestern tastes into an exciting yet casual dining experience.

The exciting menu is limited and changed regularly reflecting seasonal marketplace treats. Year-round stand-bys that rise to new gourmet heights of taste are the roast rack of lamb with Madeira sauce; roast duckling with various sauces; pan grilled range chicken with south-western sauces; and the mesquite grilled veal chop served with a mustard butter. There is always at least one fresh fish on the menu and it usually parallels the excitement of the meat and poultry dishes. During the summertime the chilled soups are notable.

A salad is a la carte, but they always have a zesty Caesar, and at least one other featuring an assortment of field greens, tomatoes and perhaps avocado, feta cheese, etc. The basket of warm rolls with blue corn muf-fins deserves a rave as do the dessert choices. The wine list offers a nice spread at reasonable prices. Table service is attentive and professional.

- **HOURS: Tues. thru Sat.: 6:00 p.m.–10:00 p.m.**
  Open for lunch
- **CLOSING DAYS: Sun. and Mon.**
- **RESERVATIONS: Yes**
- **PARKING: Lot**
- **CREDIT CARDS: All**
- **HANDICAPPED ACCESS: No difficulty**
- **AVERAGE CHECK FOR TWO: $70.00**

El Charro

311 N. Court Avenue
Tucson 622-5465

Dine in a historical Tucson home built by the father of El Charro's founder. A favorite place to eat for more than 68 years, El Charro offers Sonoran-style Mexican food at its best. This festive house is filled with family photos, brightly colored calendars, Mexican hats and rugs, baskets and hanging pottery.

Whatever your favorite Mexican dish, you will likely find some variation of it here. There are tacos, rellenos, flautas and more. The burro and chimichanga with beans and El Charro's own sun-dried carne seca are both winners. Order these "Elegante" and they arrive enchilada-style with guacamole, sour cream and lettuce! The enchiladas are not quite as massive, but just as impressive. The yellow cheese enchilada with sour cream and guacamole is outstanding and preferable to the enchiladas made with white cheese. If you have room for dessert, the deep-fried fruit twist is marvelous.

Several small touches add to the dining experience: fresh mint for the iced tea, lemon in the water, an English guide to "Restaurant Spanish" on the menu and a spicy "hot" salsa that will tantalize your tastebuds. A small "Heart Smart" menu is another great plus. Both American and Mexican beer and Inglenook wines are served. Service is friendly. This is a place for relaxed dining.

- **HOURS: Mon. thru Sun.: 4:00 p.m.–9:00 p.m.**
  Open for lunch
- **CLOSING DAYS: None** • **RESERVATIONS: 14 or more**
- **PARKING: Lot and Street** • **CREDIT CARDS: All**
- **HANDICAPPED ACCESS: Steps at front entrance**
- **AVERAGE CHECK FOR TWO: $16.00**

El Chilito

914 E. Baseline Road (Rural)
Tempe 839-5899

TEMPE

Probably the most comfortable and laid back Mexican eating place in the Valley. Only hanging serapes, Mexican hats and pottery indicate the culinary challenge. There are booths for privacy, but the luxurious easy chairs at tables make for a sweet evening.

The accent is on southern Mexican cuisine. Although they bow to gringo tastes for flautas, tamales, tostadas, chile rellenos, enchiladas, etc., and you pick any combination, the specialties of the house are more intriguing and exciting. Here you enjoy carne a la Tampiquena: Mexican beef filet with guacamole, beans, rice, chile strips and green onions. If you are a pork lover, try the carnitas de puerco with charro beans, salsa guacamole, pico de gallo and tortillas. Marinated beef Yucatan style with red chile sauce is another taste thrill. They also offer a taco platter for two where you make your own meal. They present the ingredients (ground and machaca beef, chicken, guacamole, cheese, lettuce, taco shells, etc.) and you do your own thing.

At the beginning a good spicy, hot salsa is presented with a basket of warm chips. A cheese flan dessert is nice. The Margaritas are good; the sangria bland. Table service is fast. Paper napkins are a downer.

- **HOURS: Sun. thru Thurs.: 5:00 p.m.–10:00 p.m.**
  Fri. and Sat.: 5:00 p.m.–11:00 p.m.
  Open for lunch
- **CLOSING DAYS: None**
- **RESERVATIONS: Yes**
- **PARKING: Lot**
- **CREDIT CARDS: All**
- **HANDICAPPED ACCESS: No difficulty**
- **AVERAGE CHECK FOR TWO: $18.00**

El Chorro Lodge

5550 E. Lincoln Drive
Scottsdale 948-5170

SCOTTSDALE

The desert between Camelback and Mummy Mountains is the setting for this delightful restaurant in Paradise Valley. Dinners have been served for more than 50 years in five unpretentious rooms of a converted adobe home that is unique and charming. There are three glowing and crackling fireplaces and western art decorates rustic walls. The cozy bar-lounge is intimate and romantic, and mixed drinks (and dinner, too) can be served alfresco on a lovely patio under the stars.

The chef specializes in rack of lamb and chateaubriand, which are good, but we prefer the tasty barbecue lamb ribs. The beef Stroganoff is filling and wholly satisfying. Seafood lovers should enjoy the shad roe on toast and the daily fresh fish dishes.

Following a relish dish of raw carrots, celery, etc. all entrees come with an ordinary iceberg lettuce salad that is not saved by a superior creamy Italian dressing. Warm cinnamon buns and petite poppy-sesame seeded rolls are standouts. There is a diverse, somewhat sophisticated, wine list with special French sections.

Tables are a bit crowded in the dining room but the food served is consistent. However, the setting is just delightful, and its popularity with local residents continues to shine through.

- **HOURS: Mon. thru Sun.: 6:00 p.m.–11:00 p.m.**
  Open for breakfast and lunch
- **CLOSING DAYS: Two weeks in August**
- **RESERVATIONS: Yes** • **CREDIT CARDS: All**
- **PARKING: Lot and valet**
- **HANDICAPPED ACCESS: No difficulty**
- **AVERAGE CHECK FOR TWO: $44.00**

El Rincon

Tlaquepaque Village
Highway 179
Sedona 282-4648

SEDONA

Enjoy lunch or dinner amidst the unique charm of the Tlaquepaque Village on the banks of beautiful Oak Creek. If you choose you can dine on the patio under a huge sycamore tree with the sound of Oak Creek for background music.

The menu announces that you will be served Arizona-style Mexican food, which is created by El Rincon from a blend of Navajo Indian and Mexican influences. They also boast in their advertising of serving the best Margaritas in town — and we agree with them.

The Navajo influence on the cooking creeps in with many dishes in subtle ways. But it is most evident with the sopapillas made of Navajo fry bread, and the Navajo pizza: a flat sopapilla covered with beans, enchilada or red or green chile sauce, cheese, onions, green peppers and tomato. The large size is a full meal for two or more and is very tasty. The rest of the menu is standard Mexican: tacos, enchiladas, chimichangas, burros, etc., but the Navajo influence is there. The a la carte menu is very good value unless you are into rice and refried beans. For dessert go for the amareto flan or one of the fruit chimichangas. Table service varies.

- **HOURS: Tues. thru Sat.: 11:00 a.m.–9:00 p.m.**
  Sun.: 12 noon to 5:00 p.m.
- **CLOSING DAYS: Mon.** • **RESERVATIONS: Dinner only**
- **PARKING: Lot** • **CREDIT CARDS: None**
- **HANDICAPPED ACCESS: Uneven stone patio**
- **AVERAGE CHECK FOR TWO: $17.50**

El Tovar

South Rim
Grand Canyon 638-2401

GRAND CANYON

Overlooking the awesome beauty of the Grand Canyon, the rustic El Tovar lodge is one of the hotel gems of the West. And with its timbered walls, high ceiling and pealed log braces the dining room even commands a respect of its own. Fireplaces are at both ends and from picture windows you can view the majesty of one of the great natural wonders of the world.

The menu is continental but the accent is French. Among the appetizers they serve a very nice black bean cake with sour cream and salsa, and a feuillete of asparagus and shrimp. However, the Caesar salad lacks sparkle and a nice herbal Italian dressing does not save the iceberg lettuce dinner salad. All the beef entrees, steaks, prime rib, and roast stuffed lamb loin etc. come across well, and the mesquite broiled veal chop with smoked tomato sauce is pleasing. The sauteed breast of chicken is uninteresting and the roast duck with green peppercorn sauce somehow misses the mark.

Potatoes and vegetables that accompany the meal vary daily and we have enjoyed the potatoes Boulanger and au gratin. The loaf of fresh baked bread is nice. An array of premises-baked pastries at meal end are irresistible. A basic wine list covers the essentials. Formally dressed waiters and waitresses do well.

- **HOURS: Mon. thru Sun.: 5:00 p.m.–10:00 p.m.**
  Open for breakfast, lunch; brunch on Sun.
- **CLOSING DAYS: None** • **RESERVATIONS: Yes**
- **PARKING: Hotel lot** • **CREDIT CARDS: All**
- **HANDICAPPED ACCESS: No difficulty**
- **AVERAGE CHECK FOR TWO: $46.00**

* *American*

Enchantment Resort

525 Boynton Canyon Road
Sedona 282–2900

SEDONA

The setting in Boynton Canyon is truly magnificent. The large dining room gives one a breathtaking 180-degree view of red rock scenery through a 10-foot high wall of glass. The decor is sand-peach color carried out on walls, upholstered chairs and tablecloths. Soft lighting, table candles, wall murals and trees at each end of the room complement the dramatic simplicity. Weather permitting, outdoor balcony dining is highly recommended. A talented piano player enhances the evening.

The exciting dinner menu is changed daily and reflects market availability of meats, fruits and produce. Everything is a la carte, and you usually have a choice of four appetizers, a hot and cold soup, three salads, eight to ten entrees, a half dozen desserts, and beverages including expresso and cappuccino. The kitchen takes no shortcuts in its strive to excellence. You can usually count on a good Caesar salad, plus steaks, veal, chicken, lamb and seafood dishes prepared in various ways with exotic sauces, relishes, herbs, cheeses and butters. No matter your selection, your taste buds will jump.

Desserts are made on the premises and lean toward toothsome pastries plus fresh fruits. The wine list is exemplary showing obvious care and knowledge. Table service by waiters and waitresses is erratic.

- **HOURS: Mon. thru Sun.: 6:30 p.m.–9:30 p.m.**
  Open for breakfast and lunch
- **CLOSING DAYS: None**
- **RESERVATIONS: Yes**
- **PARKING: Lot**
- **CREDIT CARDS: All**
- **HANDICAPPED ACCESS: No difficulty**
- **AVERAGE CHECK FOR TWO: $50.00**

Italian
Continental

Ernesto's Backstreet

San Angelo Square
3603 E. Indian School Road
Phoenix 957-0303

PHOENIX

A beautiful dining room, opulent and elegant, serving decent food prepared in the grand manner. Renaissance art adorns dark blue walls, mirrored chandeliers cast a soft glow on white pillars, and comfortable upholstered campaign chairs encircle candlelite tables of sparkling crystal, china and silver.

Hot garlic bread is presented to the table soon after water glasses are filled. There are six seafood dishes, 10 beef and fowl entrees, six veal creations, over a dozen pasta selections, plus soups, salads and several specials that don't make the printed list.

The tortellini Romano stuffed with fine meats, cream cheese and walnuts is a standout dish; also, the mostaccioli all' Amatriciana with ham, onion and pear tomatoes. The chef has a nice touch with veal in a variety of dishes and shrimp scampi is enjoyable. The filet of beef Casino and the bistecca Angelo are both beautiful. There are also several combinations recommended by Countess Maria Orsini that may appeal: veal and crabmeat, lamb and veal chops, etc. Both soup and salad are included with the entree.

The wine list is one of the best in the Valley with some excellent Italian vintages. The waiters usually provide smooth and competent service.

- **HOURS: Mon. thru Sun.: 5:00 p.m.–12 midnight**
  Open for lunch
- **CLOSING DAYS: None**
- **RESERVATIONS: Yes**
- **PARKING: Valet**
- **CREDIT CARDS: All**
- **HANDICAPPED ACCESS: Five steps at entrance**
- **AVERAGE CHECK FOR TWO: $38.00**

Etienne's Different Pointe of View

The Pointe at Tapatio Cliffs
11111 N. 7th Street
Phoenix 866-7500

This mountain top dining room has picture windows looking down on the twinkling lights of Phoenix. Come to luxuriate in posh surroundings, ecstacize over the sophisticated menu, enjoy haute cuisine served in the grand manner and carry away a beautiful memory of an enchanted evening.

The gourmet menu is in French with English subtitles. Hors d'oeuvres range from caviar and escargot to frog legs and goose liver pate. Both the hot dandelion salad and the salade Champagne with strips of smoked duck breast are rapturous. The generous Caesar salad is beautifully balanced with the tangy dressing always hoped for. Entrees are impressive. You can choose from poached stingray and a daily wild game selection to sauteed breast of pheasant and duck. We recommend the rack of lamb, a fantastic filet mignon capella Etienne with Maui onions and mushrooms, and fresh sauteed salmon with pink peppercorn sauce. All entrees include potatoes, vegetable du jour and beverage of your choice.

Table service by grey uniformed waiters is polished and a talented piano player enlivens the evening. Much time and effort has gone in to developing a fine wine selection from international vineyards.

- **HOURS: Mon. thru Thurs.: 6:00 p.m.–10:00 p.m.**
  Fri. and Sat.: 6:00 p.m.–11:00 p.m.
  Sunday brunch
- **CLOSING DAYS: Sun.**
- **RESERVATIONS: Yes**
- **PARKING: Lot and valet**
- **CREDIT CARDS: All**
- **HANDICAPPED ACCESS: Ramp and elevator**
- **AVERAGE CHECK FOR TWO: $75.00**

Southwestern
Mexican

NEW!

Fajitas

9841 N. Black Canyon Hwy.
Phoenix 870-4030

If you are mildly adventurous and a little bored with the commonplace, here is the place for you. It's festive and fun, very casual, perhaps a little noisy for some, but the food is great. It is, to many, a new dining experience created by southwestern range cowboys. To spice up their bland diet, the cowboys marinated skirt steak overnight and cut it into strips for broiling over a campfire.

At Fajitas, beef, chicken, pork or shrimp are seasoned to perfection and broiled over red hot mesquite in the center of the dining room. This sizzling dish is presented to each diner with onions, green pepper slices, chunky guacamole, pico de gallo tomato sauce and sour cream. Take any or all of these ingredients and place them in a fresh flour tortilla and eat "taco-style." Unlimited tortillas, made in the glass enclosed Fajitas bakery, encourages each diner to create his own combination. The warm tortillas are brought to you in a colorful, woven grass basket.

The fajitas are the only way to go, but the menu does offer standard Mexican items: tacos, enchiladas, carne asada, quesadillas and nachos. Frozen Margaritas are a specialty from a large selection of imported tequillas.

- **HOURS: Sun. thru Thurs.: 5:00 p.m.–10:30 p.m.**
  Fri. and Sat.: 5:00 p.m.–11:00 p.m.
  Open for lunch
- **CLOSING DAYS: None**
- **RESERVATIONS: Yes**
- **PARKING: Lot**
- **CREDIT CARDS: All**
- **HANDICAPPED ACCESS: No difficulty**
- **AVERAGE CHECK FOR TWO: $26.00**

Fiddlers

702 S. Milton Road
Flagstaff 774-6689

FLAGSTAFF

Here is pleasant dining in a relaxing, quiet ambience. Glass topped tables and comfortable booths, and lots of dark wood paneling create a conservative, clubby atmosphere. Soft lighting maintains the cozy theme.

The two-page menu is standard with all the popular dishes that travelers have come to expect. All the favorites are here. The only different items of gastronomic interest is a stunning Italian bocconcini, which is chicken and sausage sauteed with garlic and herbs, and baked with noodles, mozzarella and Parmesan cheeses. It is rich and filling to say the least. Fiddlers prime rib of beef (two cuts) is above average, and the steaks, filet mignon, roast loin of pork and pork chops are juicy and tasty. The veal Oscar and veal Francaise are not up to standard, and there is no special excitement in the frozen seafood, chicken dishes or the three pastas.

All entrees come with a choice of a good soup, a dull salad, mixed vegetables, and a choice of potato of the day or seasoned rice. Desserts are made on the premises but are only standard as is the limited wine list. There is a special menu for children under 12. Waitress service is adequate and table cleanup is quick.

- **HOURS:** Sun. thru Thurs.: 5:00 p.m.–9:00 p.m.
Fri. and Sat.: 5:00 p.m.–10:00 p.m.
Open for lunch
- **CLOSING DAYS:** None
- **RESERVATIONS:** Yes
- **PARKING:** Lot
- **CREDIT CARDS:** All
- **HANDICAPPED ACCESS:** No difficulty
- **AVERAGE CHECK FOR TWO:** $32.00

Fish Market

1720 E. Camelback Road
Phoenix 277-3474

PHOENIX

The spiffy interior is nautical and reminiscent of wharfside restaurants in New England with a wooden deck and big windows. Seafaring photos cover walls in addition to mounted fish caught by intrepid anglers. Picture windows look in on the immaculate kitchen and attendant activities.

The single page menu is printed daily to reflect availability of fresh seafood, and is broken down to seafood cocktails: shrimp, crab, ceviche, etc.; raw oysters and clams; baked shellfish; steamed shellfish: clams, mussels, etc.; chowders: sashimi; smoked fish: albacore, trout, salmon, etc.; oyster bar specialties: prawns, scallops, oysters, clams, etc.; pasta appetizers: a creamy fettucine with smoked salmon and green onions is phenominal; salads; and some fresh fish entrees.

All entrees include choice of tossed green salad or cup of chowder, fresh vegetables, and your choice of cottage cheese, rice, French fries, parsley or au gratin potatoes. Warm sourdough bread brings back memories of San Francisco. A modest priced wine and beer list is on the table. Service is lackadaisical. Upscale dining in a more fancy setting is on the second floor in the "Top of the Market" room.

- **HOURS: Sun. thru Thurs.: 5:00 p.m.–9:30 p.m.**
  Fri. and Sat.: 5:00 p.m.–10:00 p.m.
  Open for lunch
- **CLOSING DAYS: None**
- **RESERVATIONS: Yes**
- **PARKING: Lot**
- **CREDIT CARDS: All**
- **HANDICAPPED ACCESS: Ramps where needed**
- **AVERAGE CHECK FOR TWO: $34.00**

Italian

Franco's Trattoria

Mountain View Plaza
9619 N. Hayden Road
Scottsdale

948-6655
948-6654

SCOTTSDALE

A small neighborhood place, this is one of only a couple of Florentine trattorias in Arizona serving specialties from the Tuscan region of Italy. In a strip shopping center, the single dining room with overhead fans has only eight tables and six booths. However, the standout menu will salivate your taste buds.

The pasta list is a Florentine's dream. Savor capellini with juicy chunks of lobster, linguini with clams, shrimps, scallops, or try flat pappardelle pasta with rabbit, onions, carrots and tomatoes — all with complementary sauces. The pasta dishes average $12. Something more solid? Then go for the venison scaloppini or the veal Lombatina, which is diced veal sauteed in garlic, rosemary, hot peppers, tomatoes and raisins. The boneless loin of pork sauteed in white wine with black olives is another nifty dish. All entrees are served with steamed fresh vegetables and potato of the day. Salads are a la carte.

There are some standard Italian desserts, all good, but save space for the specialty tiramisu — a layered cake with assorted fillings. It is divine. The wine list features only Italian labels with reasonable prices. Table service by waiters in cafe aprons is fast and efficient.

- **HOURS: Mon. thru Sat.: 5:00 p.m.–10:00 p.m.**
- **CLOSING DAYS: Sun.**
- **RESERVATIONS: Yes**
- **PARKING: Shopping center lot**
- **CREDIT CARDS: AE**
- **HANDICAPPED ACCESS: No difficulty**
- **AVERAGE CHECK FOR TWO: $42.00**

French Corner

Uptown Plaza
50 E. Camelback Road
Phoenix 234-0245

PHOENIX

This is a perky little French bistro/brasserie with marble topped tables in two dining rooms with brass, glass and overhead fans. Piano music, candles and soft lights make for a romantic interlude.

The solid menu is not extensive and the kitchen does not overreach. The breast of chicken cordon bleu, frogs legs and roast rack of lamb with Dijon mustard are all enjoyable but rather pedestrian for the land of Escoffier. However, the chef hits his stride on veal sweetbreads braised in white wine, poached fresh salmon in bearnaise sauce, and N.Y. strip steak with bearnaise or green peppercorn sauce. The French fried potatoes are outstanding. The daily specials rarely disappoint.

All entrees come with fresh vegetables and a house salad with a zesty vinaigrette dressing. Other menu salads include an enjoyable ratatouille, chicken salad and a vegetarian plate — perfect for dieters. The house salad is often a great spinach salad. The special garlic cheese bread is very good. For dessert you are shown an album of color photographs, and they taste as good as they look. The wine list has been improved but prices have been kept within reason. Waiters and waitresses in green cafe aprons are alert and friendly.

- **HOURS: Mon. thru Sat.: 5:00 p.m.–12 midnight**
Open for breakfast and lunch
- **CLOSING DAYS: Sun.** • **RESERVATIONS: Yes**
- **PARKING: Shopping center lot** • **CREDIT CARDS: All**
- **HANDICAPPED ACCESS: No difficulty**
- **AVERAGE CHECK FOR TWO: $44.00**

Garcia's

A total of nine convenient locations in the Valley of the Sun. Consult your telephone directory for addresses.

PHX – SCTSDL – TEMPE – MESA – CHANDLER

Here is the magic of Mexico in the Valley of the Sun. Everything is bright, colorful and cheerful. Feel free to join the fun. The sounds of South of the Border are alive with strolling mariachis and troubadors in the bar-lounge areas.

The 10 Mexican dinner combinations are all appetizing and tasty. The tacos, flautas, enchiladas, tamales, chile rellenos, etc. are all good. However, for the neophyte to Mexican cuisine we suggest El Supremo sampler or Olivia's sampler for $7.95. Here you have a sample of most favorites — and you can go on from there! Spicy hot dishes are cooled down for more temperate American taste buds.

Two excellent dishes are (1) the pollo fundido, a deep fried, crispy flour tortilla filled with tender seasoned chicken, covered with melted cheese and served with rice; and (2) Garcia's chimichanga, a crisp burro with your favorite filling (ground or shredded beef, red or green chile, or chicken) with two crisp tortilla boats on the side filled with sour cream and guacamole. The Mexican-style rib-eye steak and sopapillas are a disappointment, but the fajitas come over well. The Margaritas are probably the best in the Valley. Table service by colorfully dressed waitresses is good.

- **HOURS: Sun. thru Thurs.: 5:00 p.m.–11:00 p.m.**
  Fri. and Sat.: 5:00 p.m.–12 midnight
  Open for lunch
- **CLOSING DAYS: None**
- **RESERVATIONS: No**
- **PARKING: Lot**
- **CREDIT CARDS: All**
- **HANDICAPPED ACCESS: No difficulty**
- **AVERAGE CHECK FOR TWO: $18.00**

* * *American*

Garden Terrace

Red Lion's La Posada Resort
4949 E. Lincoln Drive (Tatum)
Paradise Valley 952-0420

PARADISE VALLEY

Here is sophisticated dining in a beautiful two-level room that suggests quiet elegance with its comfortable chairs and soft pink glow from crystal chandeliers. Picture windows overlook Camelback Mountain and the largest resort swimming pool in Arizona. A pianist provides pleasant music.

The eclectic menu is changed periodically and the chef's scan of the seasonal provender brings off the magic of consistently exciting fare. A complimentary smoked salmon mousse appetizer is presented on being seated. Salads are a la carte and the dinner salad is beautiful dark green lettuce with a snappy dressing. Entrees include fresh vegetables and a starch of the day.

The symphony of dishes from the kitchen will make epicures swoon. Examples: ragout of sea scallops and lobster with watercress and cognac cream in a puff pastry, roast rack of lamb with three pepper cognac sauce, and breast of duck Madagascar with green peppercorn sauce and prickly pear jelly. But the basics are there also. Thus there is top sirloin and New York steaks, grilled lamb chops and roast prime rib of beef.

Desserts will make the dieters cry and others smile. Don't miss the gateau riche. The wine list is intelligent and beautifully presented. Table service is efficient.

- **HOURS: Mon. thru Sun.: 5:00 p.m.–10:00 p.m.**
  Open for breakfast, lunch; brunch on Sun.
- **CLOSING DAYS: None** • **RESERVATIONS: Yes**
- **PARKING: Lot and valet** • **CREDIT CARDS: All**
- **HANDICAPPED ACCESS: Escalators and elevators**
- **AVERAGE CHECK FOR TWO: $50.00**

Glass Door

6939 E. Main Street
Scottsdale 994-5303

SCOTTSDALE

Here is a place of style and grace, and usually solid dependability. Dining is in a recently redecorated, three-sectioned room with soft, subdued light, and is far from the lounge-bar and attendant activity.

An extensive, easy-to-read menu is an epicurean's delight with meat and seafood specialties ranging from basic (steaks and rack of lamb) to esoteric (filet of sole Florentine and veal Perigordine). Although these are all decently prepared, we recommend the Glass Door specials. These are apparently the chef's masterpieces: special lamb, special prawns, special veal, etc. as well as the Glass Door salad. The latter consists of bibb lettuce, mushrooms, heart of palm and avocado with a zesty mustard dressing. The veal Port au Prince served on sesame noodles with wine sauce, mushrooms, etc. is also tops.

The dinner price includes a choice of soup or salad (a delightful cream garlic house dressing saves an iceberg lettuce salad), potato, fresh vegetables of the day, and coffee or tea. The warm, fresh French bread is good. The desserts are the weakest part of the menu. There is a very adequate vintage wine list with California and European varieties at reasonable prices. The waiter service is merely functional: they record, deliver and bill. At times it can be slow.

- **HOURS: Mon. thru Sat.: 5:30 p.m.–11:00 p.m.**
  Open for lunch
- **CLOSING DAYS: Sun.**
- **RESERVATIONS: Yes**
- **PARKING: Valet and street**
- **CREDIT CARDS: All**
- **HANDICAPPED ACCESS: No difficulty**
- **AVERAGE CHECK FOR TWO: $38.00**

Gold Room

Westward Look Resort
245 E. Ina Road
Tucson 297-1151

TUCSON

Dine in casual elegance with a view of the city. The twinkling lights of Tucson can be seen from every vantage point in the room. Although the room is large, the fresh flowers and candles at each table add a cozy touch. Dinner music is pleasant.

For the seafood enthusiast it will be difficult to make it past the appetizers: baked oysters au gratin, snails Burgundy style, scallops with dry vermouth, avocado stuffed with crabmeat and more. The seafood entrees are equally astonishing, ranging from broiled rock lobster to scampi sauteed with garlic, onion, and sherry. All of this and the specialty of the house has yet to be revealed — veal! You may have your veal topped with crabmeat and asparagus or sauteed with shallots, dry vermouth, fresh cream and proscuitto or breaded and sauteed, etc. As if this were not enough, there are also beef, lamb and chicken dishes. Chicken fans will particularly delight in the sauteed chicken with proscuitto, cheese and spinach.

Dinners include soup du jour (scrumptious cream of cheese soup) or dark green lettuce salad (try the Italian Caesar house dressing), fresh vegetables and rice, potato or fettucine (the best there is). Desserts are sensational and the wine list is outstanding.

- **HOURS: Mon. thru Sun.: 5:30 p.m.–10:00 p.m.**
  Open for breakfast and lunch
- **CLOSING DAYS: None**
- **RESERVATIONS: Yes**
- **PARKING: Lot and valet**
- **CREDIT CARDS: All**
- **HANDICAPPED ACCESS: No difficulty**
- **AVERAGE CHECK FOR TWO: $50.00**

Golden Phoenix

6048 N. 16th Street, Phoenix 263-8049
1534 W. Camelback Rd., Phoenix 279-4447
7910 E. Chaparral Rd., Scottsdale 941-9355

PHOENIX – SCOTTSDALE

Here is Mandarin-style northern Chinese cooking with its delicate tastes and flavors combined with spicy Szechuan overtones. But most important, the food is generally reliable with over 100 items exploring the endless resources of Chinese cuisine. Each Golden Phoenix has a distinctive decor with the 16th Street place being the most luxurious. Be sure to check out that ceiling.

Many visits and comments from friends lead us to extol the chef's tasty lemon chicken and exotic curry chicken with green peppers, onions and carrots. The Kung Pao diced chicken with peanuts and spicy hot sauce is everything hoped for. Beef dishes that score high are the tasty Mongolian beef with green onions and the Peking beef with mushrooms and peanuts. Seafood lovers should stick to the shrimp presentations: the beautiful blending of shrimp and chicken with cashew nuts and the Kung Pao shrimp with that tantalizing hot spicy sauce. The complete dinners are worth reviewing and are bargain priced. Spicy dishes can be heated up or cooled down.

The white rice, tea and fortune cookies are the expected accompaniments for a Chinese meal and require no comment. Table service by fast stepping waiters and waitresses has always been good.

- **HOURS: Mon. thru Sun.: 4:00 p.m.–10:00 p.m.**
  Open for lunch
- **CLOSING DAYS: None**
- **RESERVATIONS: Yes**
- **PARKING: Lots**
- **CREDIT CARDS: All**
- **HANDICAPPED ACCESS: No difficulty**
- **AVERAGE CHECK FOR TWO: $25.00**

* * *American*

Golden Swan

Hyatt Regency Scottsdale
7500 E. Doubletree Ranch Road
Scottsdale 991-3388

SCOTTSDALE

A slick, polished bilevel dining room that delivers on food, service and ambience. Weather permitting dine outside next to the koi pond with black swans and ducks. Quality and performance is evident during every minute of your meal.

After Evian water is poured and a complimentary pre-appetizer presented, the glories of the menu can be relished. Memorable appetizers are pheasant pate with honey mustard, and wild boar sausage. Soups enjoyed include lobster bisque, various chilled fruit soups and game consumme. Of four salads the Caesar, wilted spinach and the American field salad with mustard seed dressing all make great taste impressions.

Entrees that generate excitement include lamb chops baked with pistachios and honey mustard and sea scallops with a tangerine horseradish cream and a watermelon fritter. Not to be missed is the house specialty: ranch chicken baked in clay and garnished with lemon cilantro butter. The clay shell is cracked open by the waiter and the tantalizing aroma is ecstasy. Entrees are beautifully presented. The menu is changed regularly.

The dessert tray is breathtaking, and the wine list shows care. Table service by black-tied waiters with cafe aprons is perfect.

- **HOURS: Mon. thru Sun.: 6:00 p.m.–10:30 p.m.
Open for lunch; brunch on Sunday**
- **CLOSING DAYS: None**
- **RESERVATIONS: Yes**
- **PARKING: Lot and valet**
- **CREDIT CARDS: All**
- **HANDICAPPED ACCESS: Several sets of steps**
- **AVERAGE CHECK FOR TWO: $60.00**

Greekfest

1219 E. Glendale Avenue
Phoenix 265-2990

PHOENIX

A bit of Athens has come to Phoenix. This mini-jewel in a pedestrian shopping center is short on elegance but long on authentic Greek cuisine. There are less than 20 tables in two connecting rooms with white arches and attractive wall adornments. Piped-in Greek music complements the meal.

The attractive blue menu is a veritable garden of delights. There is a great selection of salads as well as hot and cold appetizers. If you are a cheese lover don't miss the feta cheese salads or the saganaki — Kasseri cheese sauteed with olive oil, flamed at the table in brandy and doused with lemon juice. The kebobs (lamb, chicken or shrimp) are prepared with skill and come with sweet onions on skewers, and are served with fresh baked vegetables, curlied fried potatoes and a small Greek salad with that marvelous feta cheese.

Among the entrees the exohiko receives top honors. It consists of pieces of lamb, cheese and vegetables, sauteed in a light sauce, wrapped in filo pastry and baked — divine! Also the moussakas, pastitsio and rack of lamb have a certain magic.

Only Greek and American wines are served at modest prices. The Greekfest is family owned and run, and is a pure delight.

- **HOURS: Mon. thru Thurs.: 5:00 p.m.–10:00 p.m.**
  Fri. and Sat.: 5:00 p.m.–11:00 p.m.
  Open for lunch
- **CLOSING DAYS: Sun.**
- **RESERVATIONS: Yes**
- **PARKING: Shopping center lot**
- **CREDIT CARDS: All**
- **HANDICAPPED ACCESS: No difficulty**
- **AVERAGE CHECK FOR TWO: $30.00**

* * * *American*

The Grill

Ritz-Carlton Hotel
2401 E. Camelback Road
Phoenix 468-0700

PHOENIX

Very clubby, somewhat masculine in tone, with polished brass chandeliers and comfortable armchairs, this is the less pretentious companion to the more elegant Restaurant next door. However, there is only one kitchen, many items appear on both menus, and the prices are the same.

As in the Restaurant, the food is up-scale American with continental finesse, but somehow broader in scope and a little more adventuresome. The lobster and pumpkin chowder is indeed splendid. Ditto the appetizer sauteed crabcake with chile-pepper relish and the fricasse of escargot with mushrooms. For entrees the Cornish game hen with cranberry butter sauce and the seafood mixed grill are both real treats worth reordering on another visit. There are also three steaks with an array of sauces, excellent roast prime rib of beef and a daily selection of fresh fish—broiled, sauteed and grilled. The dinner rolls can still be improved.

The dessert tray is gorgeous with the Bailly's Irish Cream cheesecake a real knockout. The wine list will satisfy the most exacting oenophile. Table service by black-tied waiters is perfect and the performance never falters. Delightful piano music from the adjoining lounge filters in unobtrusively.

- **HOURS: Tues. thru Sun.: 6:00 p.m.–10:00 p.m.**
  Open for lunch
- **CLOSING DAYS: Mon.**
- **RESERVATIONS: Yes**
- **PARKING: Lot, garage and valet**
- **CREDIT CARDS: All**
- **HANDICAPPED ACCESS: No difficulty**
- **AVERAGE CHECK FOR TWO: $65.00**

*

Cuban
Spanish

Havana Cafe

4225 E. Camelback Road
Phoenix

952-1991

PHOENIX

One of the smallest restaurants in Arizona, this cozy place is intimate and enjoyable with brass accents, a mirrored wall and unobtrusive piped-in Spanish music. A small bar in the corner breaks up the grey walls. Although the setting is modest the cuisine is exciting, memorable and inspirational.

The wonderful bill of fare boasts of traditional Cuban and Spanish dishes, and everything is a la carte. An absolute must is the robust, black bean soup, the national soup of Cuba. Two other soups vary daily and also rate high. Another must is the roast fresh leg of pork seasoned with sour orange, herbs and sherry wine. Any of the five Cuban-style steaks marinated with lime juice and spices are also standouts. The various chicken and seafood dishes deserve special raves. Ditto the dark green lettuce dinner salad. The creamy rice pudding, bread pudding with chocolate sauce and the Spanish custard are all grande finales to a memorable repast.

Waiters in black pants, white shirts and bow ties are competent and professional. The menu states, "No Smoking in the Dining Roon." Limited parking in the small lot can be a problem on a busy night.

- **HOURS: Mon. thru Sat.: 5:00 p.m.–10:00 p.m.**
  Open for lunch
- **CLOSING DAYS: Sun.**
- **RESERVATIONS: No**
- **PARKING: Lot**
- **CREDIT CARDS: MC, V**
- **HANDICAPPED ACCESS: No difficulty**
- **AVERAGE CHECK FOR TWO: $32.00**

American

Hidden Garden

1610 W. Highway 89-A
Sedona

282-6667

SEDONA

Welcome to "Grandma's Tearoom." It is just as you remember it — or envision it. Dried flowers, colorful paintings and bric-a-brac make this a very cozy, cute dining room. Fresh flowers adorn tables surrounded by upholstered antique chairs, of which no two are alike. A full service bar is in one corner. Weather permitting, al fresco dining is enjoyed on metal garden furniture in a semi-covered outdoor patio.

The pink, single page bill of fare is simplicity itself: only five appetizers and nine entrees. The chef does not overreach, and obviously concentrates his/her talents on just those special dishes. Indeed, the loin lamb chops with pear chutney, and the broiled trout with peppers, mushrooms and onion sauteed in wine come over well. The N.Y. steak with roasted garlic butter and the grilled citrus chicken also hit the mark. Smaller appetites should go for the Alaskan king crab or smoked salmon quesadillas. The Caesar salad lacks bite.

Entrees come with a choice of a daily, fresh-made soup or a good, dark green lettuce salad with a choice of tangy dressings. The homemade carrot cake is the best of an array of rich desserts. The wine list is standard. Waitress table service can often be slow.

- **HOURS: Thurs. thru Tues.: 5:30 p.m.–9:00 p.m.**
  Open for breakfast, lunch and afternoon tea
- **CLOSING DAYS: Wed.**
- **RESERVATIONS: Yes**
- **PARKING: Lot**
- **CREDIT CARDS: MC, V**
- **HANDICAPPED ACCESS: No difficulty**
- **AVERAGE CHECK FOR TWO: $28.00**

Italian
American

Hops

Scottsdale Fashion Square
7000 E. Camelback Road
Scottsdale

945-4677

SCOTTSDALE

A large, barn-like room with dining on two levels and outdoors, this is a showcase restaurant for a mini-brewery. The ceiling is unfinished exposing rafters, vent-pipes and cables. There is nothing to buffer sound so the place is very noisy. In spite of the very informal, high decibel atmosphere the food is good.

The single page, plasticized menu accents a modest array of snacks, appetizers, starters, pizzas and calzone (a stuffed, Italian, deep fried, puff pastry) which go well with a glass of premises-brewed suds. The smoked salmon cakes and the mixed grill K-bobs with peanut sauce are delightful. The quesadillas and peel-and-eat shrimp are also enjoyable. Six pizzas from all-veggie to carmelized onion and spicy chicken will awaken dormant taste buds.

If you wish to go beyond yuppie snacking, then peruse the list of nine enticing entrees. The daily fresh fish, including salmon and swordfish, have always been beyond reproach. The roast chicken Margarita has a nice zing to it. The prime rib and the N.Y. strip steak are better ordered elsewhere. The dark green lettuce salad and the Caesar are both great. Table service can be very erratic.

- **HOURS** **Sun. thru Thus.: 5:30 p.m.–10:30 p.m.**
  Fri. and Sat.: 5:30 p.m.–11:00 p.m.
  Open for lunch
- **CLOSING DAYS: None**
- **RESERVATIONS: Yes**
- **PARKING: Lot**
- **CREDIT CARDS: All**
- **HANDICAPPED ACCESS: No difficulty**
- **AVERAGE CHECK FOR TWO: $30.00**

House of Joy

Hull Avenue
Jerome
634-5339

JEROME

An old bordello that provided joy to miners in bygone days now provides gastronomic joy to visitors in this resurrected ghost town. Two dining rooms with only seven tables on the ground floor have red lights, abundant bric-a-brac, old photos, antique furniture and memorabilia.

The bill of fare is choice but limited in scope. There is a talented handling of veal in four dishes: cordon bleu, and scalloppini — lemon, Marsala or sherry. The herbed lamb or lamb topped with curry sauce is not to be missed and the Cornish game hen, either Kiev or cordon bleu is satisfying. The fish dishes fluctuate from excellent to bland, the halibut on a recent visit was perfection. There is no beef on the menu, so steak and prime rib lovers should dine elsewhere.

All entrees include an outstanding warm, home-made bread, delicious soup, a fresh but unimaginative tossed green salad, superb hot muffins (the sour cream cherry variety are ephemeral!), stuffed baked potato with cheese and a fresh vegetable. Home baked desserts vary each weekend and are always superlative productions.

The wine list is limited but adequate. Table service is genial. NOTE: reservations must be made several weeks in advance. This is a very popular place and, as stated on a sign at the front door, "If you don't have reservations, don't come in."

- **HOURS: Sat. and Sun. only: 3:00 p.m.–9:00 p.m.**
- **CLOSING DAYS: Mon. thru Fri.**
- **RESERVATIONS: Yes**
- **PARKING: Street**
- **CREDIT CARDS: None**
- **HANDICAPPED ACCESS: No difficulty**
- **AVERAGE CHECK FOR TWO: $38.00**

Houston's

2425 E. Camelback Road
Phoenix

957-9700

There is a delightful informality about the pleasures of eating and drinking in this bustling place. The two level dining room is all booths with an open kitchen on one side and a busy bar opposite. A green wall clock circled by pink neon is the outstanding decorative feature. The noise level is high, so outside patio dining has its attraction.

In spite of the clamorous turmult, and a ketchup bottle on every table, the food is good — even brilliant. The chicken dishes are all superlative productions with the Santa Fe platter an edible symphony. Two or three daily fresh fish dishes also ring the bell. The prime rib deserves a rave, but the strip sirloin and filet mignon miss the mark. Appetizers and extras are superb: creamy cole slaw, iron skillet beans, cheese toast, creamed spinach with artichoke, etc. Salads are a la carte, fresh made and satisfying.

Houston's serves no bread, rolls or butter except what comes with a couple of entrees. Desserts are limited to an exemplary daily fruit cobbler with ice cream, and a rich, five-nut brownie with ice cream and Kahlua. Table service by waiters and waitresses is erratic. East parking lot is a hike; try underground.

- **HOURS: Sun. thru Thurs.: 4:00 p.m.–11:00 p.m.**
  Fri. and Sat.: 4:00 p.m.–12 midnight
- **CLOSING DAYS: None**
- **RESERVATIONS: No**
- **PARKING: Lots and garage**
- **CREDIT CARDS: All**
- **HANDICAPPED ACCESS: No difficulty**
- **AVERAGE CHECK FOR TWO: $35.00**

Humphreys

1405 W. Highway 89-A
Sedona 282-7745

SEDONA

For the best selection of seafood dishes in the Red Rock country, Humphreys' is the place. Although seemingly an afterthought, a small selection of steaks rates high. This popular eating spot is family owned and operated, and they try to add the personal touch to table service. The spacious, airy, blue walled dining room is comfortable and cozy with glass topped tables and booths.

The fish choices are both fresh and frozen, and range from orange roughy, Pacific snapper, halibut and mahi-mahi to rainbow trout and catfish. Shellfish offerings include lobster, king crablegs and shrimp. The latter come either grilled, deep fried or in a bowl for hand peeling and eating. All are properly prepared, tasty and enjoyable. The entrees can be prepared with or without butter or special sauces, of which you have a choice. The New York strip is your best steak bet.

With all entrees you receive a choice of a good daily soup or a dull iceberg lettuce salad, bread or rolls, and a choice of an acceptable rice, baked potato or potato of the day. Desserts offer little in the way of excitement. The wine list offers the basics at moderate prices. Table service is usually smooth and efficient. PIped-in music adds a pleasant touch.

- **HOURS: Mon. thru Sun.: 5:00 p.m.–9:30 p.m.**
  Open for lunch
- **CLOSING DAYS: None**
- **RESERVATIONS: Yes**
- **PARKING: Lot**
- **CREDIT CARDS: MC, V**
- **HANDICAPPED ACCESS: No difficulty**
- **AVERAGE CHECK FOR TWO: $30.00**

Hunan

1575 E. Camelback Road
Phoenix 265-9484

PHOENIX

Here you savor the authentic country-style cooking of southern China. Although the accent is on the cuisine of Hunan, there are also some Szechuan spicy-hot classics as well as sophisticated Mandarin entrees and a couple of Korean dishes. The exciting menu has nine creative oriental specialties that were first served in Phoenix by the Hunan — and they will challenge your powers of decision. They also have Shanghai style cooking with light, crispy coatings for chicken, duck and seafood dishes.

The dining room is bright and light with crisp white tablecloths and fast-stepping waiters. The shrimp, beef and chicken Tsao San Shien, the sea scallops with garlic, and the Hunan lamb in hot sauce are all particularly enjoyable. Other memorable delights are beef and chicken Hunan style, as well as moo shu pork in crepes.

In addition to the specialty dishes, there is a flavorful shredded beef, sauteed Szechuan style, Mandarin spicy shrimps, and an aromatic Mongolian pork with green onions in Mongolian sauce. With each entree comes a large plate of steamed rice. All spicy hot dishes are marked on the menu and can be modified to individual tastes. Plum sauce is conveniently available from a help-yourself jar on the table.

- **HOURS: Sun. thru Thurs.: 5:00 p.m.–10:00 p.m.**
  Fri. and Sat.: 5:00 p.m.–11:00 p.m.
  Open for lunch
- **CLOSING DAYS: None**
- **RESERVATIONS: Yes**
- **PARKING: Lot**
- **CREDIT CARDS: All**
- **HANDICAPPED ACCESS: One small step at front door**
- **AVERAGE CHECK FOR TWO: $18.00**

Hungry Hunter

A total of four convenient locations in the Valley of the Sun and one in Yuma. Consult your telephone directory for addresses.

PHOENIX – SCOTTSDALE – TEMPE – YUMA

Brass, glass and dark woods, these restaurants are warm and inviting with fireplaces (albeit artificial), soft music, macrame hanging plants, and comfortable tables and booths. These are commercially quaint places that come off rather well.

The Hungry Hunters specialize in beef, and there is a choice of 10 steaks, filets and three cuts of prime rib (petite, standard and house). The steaks are good for the price, and the roast beef is among the best in Arizona. The waiter will announce the fresh fish items of the day, which are off-menu and usually good. There are also frozen seafood entrees ranging from salmon and swordfish to shrimp, crab legs and lobster tails. Of course, there are all kinds of steak and seafood combinations.

With each entree you receive a cup of soup, a salad selection brought to your table, an excellent, hot, whole wheat bread loaf, plus your choice of a baked potato, red skinned potatoes or rice pilaf. The dessert tray is sinful. Table service is smooth and easy, and there is a well-presented wine list. Twilight dining before 6:00 p.m. is a real bargain.

- **HOURS: Mon. thru Thurs.: 5:00 p.m.–10:00 p.m.**
  Fri. and Sat.: 5:00 p.m.–11:00 p.m.
  Sun.: 4:00 p.m.–10:00 p.m.
  Open for lunch
- **CLOSING DAYS: None** • **RESERVATIONS: Over six**
- **PARKING: Lots** • **CREDIT CARDS: All**
- **HANDICAPPED ACCESS: No difficulty**
- **AVERAGE CHECK FOR TWO: $32.00**

* * *Italian*

Ianuzzi Ristorante

El Pedregal at the Boulders
34505 N. Scottsdale Road
Scottsdale 488-4141

SCOTTSDALE

Welcome to Ianuzzi's latest adventure in fine dining with great food, meticulous service, personal comfort and a seductive view of the shimmering lights of Paradise Valley. The splendid menu is lavish and reflects Ianuzzi's classic adherence to quality and tradition. Weather permitting dining on an outdoor balcony adds a special romance to the magic of the evening.

The fare is basically Italian, broad in scope, and always delicious with gourmet flair and style. The pasta list goes from the simple to the sublime. The fettucine Alfredo with pieces of smoked salmon, caviar, vodka, cream and peppercorns is a dish to dream on. The chef has a fine touch with chicken dishes, and the roasted garlicked chicken with potatoes and chestnuts, and the boneless chicken with golden raisins, pine nuts and nutmeg are two great examples. The veal, beef and seafood creations also pass muster.

Along with Italian bread, wrapped breadsticks are a nice touch. The mixed lettuce salad with a snappy vinaigrette is above reproach; the Caesar and spinach salads are good. The wine list is limited to Italian, German and California bottlings but has depth and range. Table service is attentive and professional. Taped music soothes the evening.

- **HOURS: Mon. thru Sun.: 5:00 p.m.–10:30 p.m.**
  Open for lunch
- **CLOSING DAYS: None**
- **RESERVATIONS: Yes**
- **PARKING: Lot**
- **CREDIT CARDS: All**
- **HANDICAPPED ACCESS: Use elevator to 2nd floor**
- **AVERAGE CHECK FOR TWO: $48.00**

* *

Southwestern Continental

Janos

150 N. Main Avenue
Tucson

884-9426

TUCSON

For the special night or as a prelude to an evening of culture, Janos provides just the right touch of class. Situated behind the Tucson Museum of Art, this gem is housed primarily in an old territorial home that boasts of sahuaro beamed ceilings and fine wood floors. The three peach tone rooms are tastefully appointed in a "less is more" decor that includes original artwork, peach napery, white dishes and peach tinted stemware. Janos has received the Mobil 4-Star Award.

Two menus are offered: Menu of the season and menu of the evening. Selections range from lobster with papaya and champagne to lamb noisettes. For duck fans the duckling with orange and green peppercorn sauce is an excellent choice. Other tantalizing dishes are the hickory smoked beef tenderloin with black beans, pan fried pecan-breaded cabrilla, sauteed veal with morels, and veal with pink peppercorns and caviar. There is also likely to be a special of the day, depending upon what is fresh and available.

Dinners include a crisp salad, small freshly baked rolls and beautifully presented vegetables. After dinner a pastry tray arrives with several homemade desserts that are truly irresistible. The wine selections include five house wines and a full range of better domestic and European vintages. Service can be erratic.

- **HOURS: Mon. thru Sat.: 5:30 p.m.–9:30 p.m.**
- **CLOSING DAYS: Sun.**
- **RESERVATIONS: Yes**
- **PARKING: Lot**
- **CREDIT CARDS: All**
- **HANDICAPPED ACCESS: Ramps**
- **AVERAGE CHECK FOR TWO: $55.00**

Jean-Claude's Petit Cafe

7340 E. Shoeman Lane   947-5194
Scottsdale   947-5288

SCOTTSDALE

Here is a rare gem — elegant dining yet comfortable and relaxing. The monastic feeling of the white stucco rooms is softened by areca palms. Colorful food posters break the monotony of the walls. Candlelit tables are immaculate with white napery, fine stemware and silver. Regrettably the table chairs are a bit uncomfortable.

The menu is modest as are the prices — not overreaching. The accent is French but there are four pasta dishes, which add an Italian overtone to the bill of fare. A couple of daily chef's specials are offered, usually in the fresh fish category. Compared to other French restaurants, Jean-Claude puts a greater accent on fresh fish dishes and they all come over well. In fact, the fish creations and the grilled loin of lamb with rosemary ginger sauce are the kitchen strongpoints.

All entrees are served with two fresh crunchy vegetables, an outstanding warm, crusty French bread, and a small crock of unsalted butter. The a la carte house salad with a vibrant mustardy vinaigrette, and the Caesar and spinach salads, are basic and good. Both the raspberry and chocolate souffles are outstanding, and the flourless chocolate cake deserves a medal. The wine list is limited but choice; table service is irregular.

- **HOURS: Mon. thru Sat.: 6:00 p.m.–10:30 p.m.**
  Open for lunch
- **CLOSING DAYS: Sun.**
- **RESERVATIONS: Yes**
- **PARKING: Street**
- **CREDIT CARDS: All**
- **HANDICAPPED ACCESS: Four low steps at entrance and a small ramp inside**
- **AVERAGE CHECK FOR TWO: $45.00**

Jerome's

6958 E. Tanque Verde Road
Tucson 721-0311

TUCSON

This is Cajun country and the culinary awards of chef Jerry Soldevery displayed in the foyer confirm that you have arrived at the right place. The decor is elegant country with dark wood walls and tables, blue chintz curtains, ceiling fans and fabric covered booths.

The appetizers offer an array of seafood delights ranging from chilled gulf oysters to Cajun seafood gumbo and barbecued shrimp. The accent now is more on seafoods than Cajun, which was a short-lived culinary fad from Louisiana. We have particularly enjoyed the veal "Tanque Verde" with spinach, the poached or mesquite grilled salmon filet with rosemary peppercorn butter, catfish "Louis," sweetwater barbeque duck, and Sonoran veal ribs with prickly pear glaze, and all the fresh fish items. The certified Angus beef steaks have never disappointed.

Dinners are served with fresh bread, vegetables, red beans, potatoes or rice and a memorable salad of green and red leaf lettuce with sunflower seeds. The house dressings, herbal cream or honey and lemon, are sensational. A number of the entree accompaniments, including the salad dressings, zucchini bread (delicious) and Louisiana wild pecan rice, may be purchased in the foyer. Desserts and breads are baked and prepared on the premises. The wine list is limited but sufficient. Service is friendly.

- **HOURS: Tues. thru Thurs. & Sun.: 5:00 p.m.–10:00 p.m.**
  Fri. & Sat.: 5:00 p.m.–11:00 p.m.
  Open for lunch; brunch on Sunday
- **CLOSING DAYS: Mon.**
- **RESERVATIONS: Yes**
- **PARKING: Lots**
- **CREDIT CARDS: All**
- **HANDICAPPED ACCESS: Ramps; no difficulty**
- **AVERAGE CHECK FOR TWO: $35.00**

Jewel of the Crown

5029 N. 44th Street (Camelback)
Phoenix 840-2412

PHOENIX

Exotic food and clean, crisp surroundings mark the leading Indian restaurant in a state where basic meat and potato fare is the norm. For the moderately adventuresome diner this is a great place to taste-test and introduce yourself to one of the world's greatest but least understood cuisines. And have no doubt about it, the popularity of Indian cuisine in the U.S.A. is growing.

There is more to Indian cuisine than curry dishes, and on scanning the menu you quickly recognize that it is a special combination of subtle spices that makes this ethnic fare so distinctive. A detailed description of each dish is given as are the ingredients. You are also alerted that the food can be served mild, medium or spicy hot — your choice.

This is the place for lamb and chicken, and all tandoori dishes baked in the clay oven on mesquite charcoal are recommended without reservation. All the curry dishes will satisfy. There is a great selection of vegetarian specialties with the tandoori roasted eggplant (bharta makhni) being edible poetry. Do not miss out on one of the unique breads with various spices. Waiter service is efficient and helpful in explaining the various dishes. Beers, wines and cocktails are also served. Both indoor and patio dining is available.

- **HOURS: Mon. thru Sun.: 5:00 p.m.–10:00 p.m.**
  Open for lunch
- **CLOSING DAYS: None** • **RESERVATIONS: Yes**
- **PARKING: Shopping center lot** • **CREDIT CARDS: All**
- **HANDICAPPED ACCESS: Use East parking lot**
- **AVERAGE CHECK FOR TWO: $35.00**

Kous Kooz (Eddie's Grill)

Valley Commerce Center
4747 N. 7th Street (Camelback Rd.)
Phoenix 241-1188

PHOENIX

For the food of today this is the current "in" place for avante garde cuisine in Phoenix. Semi-surrounded by Japanese koi ponds, this modernistic dining room will grab your attention. There are neon accents and two bright, bas relief silhouettes that are artfully backlighted. Quiet it is not; exciting and noisy it is.

The restaurant boasts of Ameriterranean cuisine: regional American favorites blended with the flavors of the Mediterranean. Thus most entrees come with either couscous, tabouli, harissa, kusa and yogurt. There is a heavy use of herbs and spices. However, the sum of the parts is exotic. Nearly all dishes soar to new heights of gourmet splendor. The seared venison, grilled salmon with black beans and goat cheese marinated grilled swordfish, Ameriterranean stew, baked lemon-mint lamb chops, the Spanish paella and the sesame seared ahi tuna are edible poetry.

All entrees come with fresh made, herbed bread called *foccacia,* and a nice dark green salad. There is no butter served or used in the restaurant. Instead you get a ramekin of olive oil with herbs and garlic to dip the bread. It's great. Desserts are fabulous, the wine list excellent and table service professional.

- **HOURS: Sun. thru Thurs.: 5:00 p.m.–10:00 p.m.**
  Fri. and Sat.: 5:00 p.m.–11:00 p.m.
  Open for lunch
- **CLOSING DAYS: None**
- **RESERVATIONS: Yes**
- **PARKING: Lot**
- **CREDIT CARDS: All**
- **HANDICAPPED ACCESS: No difficulty**
- **AVERAGE CHECK FOR TWO: $60.00**

Kyoto

7170 E. Stetson Drive (Scottsdale Road)
Scottsdale 990-9374

SCOTTSDALE

A plain functional restaurant, rather typical of suburban Tokyo places, but lacking the authenticity in food quality and preparation. But all is not bad. When the raw tuna, yellow tail and eel are fresh, and of premium grade, excellent sushi can be had at reasonable prices. The sushi bar will hold 12 and is the best reason for visiting the Kyoto.

More atuned to western tastes are the steak, chicken, shrimp, scallops and lobster prepared at square teppanyaki tables. Here is theatrical dining where the teppan chef twirls and spins his knives to cut and slice meats, seafood, mushrooms and onions with a flair of the martial arts. There are special tables with the grill in the center. Regrettably, you must often wait until your eight-place table is filled before the chef starts his performance. But the tasty grilled tidbits are worth the wait besides being lots of fun.

Vegetables, fish and shrimp are also available tempura style. These light battered, deep fried lacy morsels come over well but somehow lack the effervescent sparkle our memory retains of tempura bars in Tokyo. The saki at Kyoto is excellent as is the Japanese beer. Table service is smooth and efficient.

- **HOURS: Sun. thru Thurs.: 5:30 p.m.–10:00 p.m.**
  Fri. and Sat.: 5:30 p.m.–11:00 p.m.
  Open for lunch
- **CLOSING DAYS: None**
- **RESERVATIONS: Yes**
- **PARKING: Street and lot**
- **CREDIT CARDS: All**
- **HANDICAPPED ACCESS: No difficulty**
- **AVERAGE CHECK FOR TWO: $30.00**

La Bruschetta

4515 N. Scottsdale Road (Camelback Rd.)
Scottsdale 946-7236

SCOTTSDALE

The emphasis is on the cuisine of the Italian region of Tuscany and its unique dishes. So indulge and delight in the culinary splendor of an array of pasta, veal, beef, chicken and seafood entrees that are memorable. On the theory that less is more, the decor is minimal with bare, off-white walls accenting the perfection of beautifully set tables and the glorious repasts thereon. A couple of large earthen jars and fresh flowers complete the scene.

On being seated you are served warm buttered toast with herbed tomato slices. Next we urge you to partake at a stunning antipasto table with a variety of fresh seafood and vegetable appetizers. The two-page menu that follows is choice and hunger satisfying. Of seven pasta dishes one marvelous creation is maccheroni baked with prosciutto ham, peas, porcini mushrooms and cream. A breast of chicken sauteed with ricotta cheese and walnuts is another standout. Also enjoyable are prawns sauteed with asparagus and chopped tomato in a cream sauce.

Salads are a la carte and there are four available. For a different dessert do not miss the fresh baked, almond-pecan cookies that you dip into a ramekin of sherry wine. Table service is perfect.

- **HOURS: Mon. thru Sun.: 5:30 p.m.–12 midnight**
- **CLOSING DAYS: None**
- **RESERVATIONS: Yes**
- **PARKING: Lot in rear**
- **CREDIT CARDS: All**
- **HANDICAPPED ACCESS: No difficulty**
- **AVERAGE CHECK FOR TWO: $55.00**

American Continental

La Champagne

Registry Resort
7171 N. Scottsdale Road
Scottsdale 991-3800

SCOTTSDALE

Trimly stylish and sophisticated, go to be dazzled by the decor as much as to enjoy the cuisine, nicely prepared and served with style.

The enchanting menu is solidly superb and is changed seasonally. The hot and cold appetizers, whether escargots or quail stuffed with pistachios, are perfection defined and are as stunning to see as to savor. The spinach and La Champagne garden salads are perfect. Among the exquisitely prepared entrees there is rack of lamb with varying sauces, succulent, juicy chateaubriand (for two) and a sensational linguini with clams and a cream sauce. There are also chicken, duck, veal and some intriguing seafood creations. With changing menus they have often added some southwestern touches such as swordfish with ancho guacamole, salmon steak with avocado-corn salsa, and grilled free range chicken with mustard seeds and coriander. The delights served on Wedgewood bone china seemingly never end. Waist stretching desserts include fresh fruits with liqueurs, chocolate mousse, cakes and pastries. Try the souffles — they are excellent.

A talented pianist plays relaxing music. Table service is deft and efficient. An extensive array of French wines including many older vintages are offered, as well as some of California's better labels.

- **HOURS: Mon. thru Sun.: 6:00 p.m.–11:00 p.m.**
- **CLOSING DAYS: Sun. and Mon. during summer**
- **RESERVATIONS: Yes**
- **PARKING: Valet and hotel lot** • **CREDIT CARDS: All**
- **HANDICAPPED ACCESS: No difficulty**
- **AVERAGE CHECK FOR TWO: $55.00**

La Chaumiere

6910 Main Street
Scottsdale 946-5115

SCOTTSDALE

Here is the look and mood of a French countryside inn with cozy touches like a massive stone hearth and a collection of culinary artifacts. The menu is a Gallic dream and the wine list fascinating.

The smoked shrimp and escargot appetizers are outstanding. The French onion and Vichyssoise soups are tops. The Caesar salad, endive salad with hazelnut oil, watercress salad and heart of Boston lettuce with vinaigrette are all tangy and perfect. There are several standout fish dishes with the filet of sole deserving a Blue Ribbon. Another epicurean dish is an opulent rack of lamb that receives wide acclaim from the locals. Other culinary creations that won't disappoint are the veal Normande, duck with either orange or cherry sauce, and the steak au poivre with green peppercorns, cognac and cream. Complete dinners include a delightful daily soup or an enjoyable salad du jour, warm French bread, garden fresh vegetables and potato of the day.

The chocolate mousse meringue cake for dessert is outstanding, and the fresh fruit tarts are worth a try. Table service is professional.

- **HOURS: Mon. thru Sat.: 5:30 p.m.–11:00 p.m.**
  Sun.: 5:00 p.m.–10:00 p.m.
  Open for lunch during winter months
- **CLOSING DAYS: Suns., May thru Dec.; and July through August**
- **RESERVATIONS: Yes**
- **PARKING: Street and valet**
- **CREDIT CARDS: All**
- **HANDICAPPED ACCESS: Three steps to main dining room; no difficulty to La Jardin Room**
- **AVERAGE CHECK FOR TWO: $60.00**

La Fontanella

4231 E. Indian School Road
Phoenix 955-1213

PHOENIX

Here is an unpretentious but beguiling restaurant with a continental cafe ambience of embracing charm. A service bar is at the entrance. The dining room has art and antiques on the walls, attractively set tables with bentwood armchairs, and fresh flowers.

The seductive menu is limited, but strict culinary discipline in the kitchen makes for no disappointments. When they have them the stuffed mushrooms appetizer is a dreamy delight. The timeless veal dishes, scaloppini, saltimbocca, Parmigiana, cacciatore, etc., are all offered with care and confidence. In fact, the veal Parmigiana with tender mushrooms, zesty tomato sauce and aromatic Parmesan cheese is probably the best in the Valley. The eight pasta dishes have been without fault. We have also enjoyed scampi, calamari Romano, several chicken dishes, the shrimp appetitoso with pine nuts over linguini and the rack of lamb Isabella.

All entrees include a good soup or an excellent mixed lettuce salad of crunchy perfection with a robust creamy Italian dressing, fresh vegetables and crusty, hot rolls with garlic herb butter. The dessert selections have improved with the addition of gelatos and tartufos. Only Italian vintages grace the wine list but prices are uncommonly fair. Waiter service is efficient.

- HOURS: **Tues. thru Sun.: 4:30 p.m.–10:00 p.m.**
  Open for lunch
- CLOSING DAYS: **Mon. and month of August**
- RESERVATIONS: **Yes** • CREDIT CARDS: **All**
- PARKING: **Small lot plus parking lot next door**
- HANDICAPPED ACCESS: **No difficulty**
- AVERAGE CHECK FOR TWO: **$30.00**

La Hacienda

Scottsdale Princess Resort
7575 E. Princess Drive
Scottsdale 585-4848

SCOTTSDALE

This is sophisticated South-of-the-Border dining like you experience in the swank Zona Rosada of Mexico City. It is fancy food and fancy prices. There is no comparison with the slap-dash, noisy taco parlors that typify so many Mexican restaurants in Arizona. Do not expect to see plain tacos, tamales, burros, tostadas or refried beans on the menu. The closest they come is the early presentation of hot tortilla chips with a zesty chunky salsa and a tasty bean dip. However, you do get comfortable surroundings, antique-style dinnerware and glassware, a quartet of mariachi troubadors, — and great food.

The kitchen's culinary efforts are really Mexican-Southwestern. Thus, enjoy mole poblano, seasoned chocolate sauce with sesame seeds and chili on a half roasted chicken, stuffed sea bass with crabmeat and lime mayonaise, roasted quail stuffed with chorizo sausage, rack of lamb roasted with chili guajillo, and tenderloin of beef glazed with Chihuahua cheese and chipote salsa. The menu highlight is the impressive spit roast suckling pig. There is a separate menu for desserts and specialty coffees. The wine and cocktail list is quite good, but table service can be erratic.

- **HOURS:** **Sun. thru Thurs.: 6:00 p.m.–10:00 p.m.**
  Fri. and Sat.: 6:00 p.m.–11:00 p.m.
  Open for lunch in winter season
- **CLOSING DAYS: None** • **RESERVATIONS: Yes**
- **PARKING: Hotel lot and valet** • **CREDIT CARDS: All**
- **HANDICAPPED ACCESS: No difficulty**
- **AVERAGE CHECK FOR TWO: $40.00**

* * *French*

La Marmite

7210 Elbow Bend Road
Carefree 488-3992

CAREFREE

Here is relaxed casual dining in the colorful living desert only 15 miles north of Scottsdale. The two level dining room has both massive black vinyl booths as well as immaculately set tables and comfortable red vinyl armchairs. Quiet piped-in French music sets the mood for dinner enjoyment.

The menu is simple and uncluttered. There are three soups and three salads that include a zippy Caesar, a tomato with cucumbers and a notable romaine lettuce house salad kissed with a tangy vinaigrette or bleu cheese dressing. The entree list breaks no new culinary ground but most dishes are deserving of acclaim. The tender breast of chicken in cream, and the shrimps in a sauce of champagne, cognac and cream are exciting. The fresh filet of sole almondine is buttery and tasty. The sweetbreads with rice, mushrooms and Madeira wine come over well, as do the three filet mignons with green peppercorns in a sauce of cognac and cream.

All dinners come with a replenished bread basket and sweet butter, choice of premises-made soup or house salad, and fresh daily vegetables. Desserts are spectacular. Table service by formally dressed waiters and waitresses is usually perfect. The wine list has some nice choices and prices are within reason.

- **HOURS: Mon. thru Sat.: 6:00 p.m.–10:00 p.m.**
- **CLOSING DAYS: Sun. and months of July and Aug.**
- **RESERVATIONS: Yes** • **PARKING: Lot**
- **CREDIT CARDS: All**
- **HANDICAPPED ACCESS: No difficulty**
- **AVERAGE CHECK FOR TWO: $40.00**

La Parrilla Suiza

3508 W. Peoria Ave., Phoenix	978-8334
5602 E. Speedway Blvd., Tucson	747-4838
2720 N. Oracle Road, Tucson	624-4300

PHOENIX – TUCSON

For a novel taste of Mexico — not the typical border fare so popularized in Arizona — these are the places. Phoenix and Tucson boast the only La Parrilla Suizas in the States with the other 22 in Mexico City, Guadalajara and Cuernavaca, Mexico. A bustling, casual setting filled with brick and greenery creates a cheery atmosphere.

The distinctiveness of the menu items lies in the preparation. The meats and cheeses are charcoal-broiled on a large grill in the middle of the restaurant. There are several taste-tempting appetizers all made with charcoal melted cheese and fresh handmade tortillas. The star attractions are tacos, chilaquiles, and meat and cheese specialties. The alambre de res made of corn tortillas covered with sauteed beef fillet, bacon, onions and bell peppers is definitely a taco delight—likewise the parilla chicken melt, which is unique to the States. The specialties which include diced, broiled sirloin are also a good bet. The charro beans served with the dinners are worth the trip themselves.

The smooth Margaritas serve as a handy accompaniment to the spicy hot enchilada sauce. Imported, domestic and Mexican beers are also available.

- **HOURS: Mon. thru Thurs.: 4:00 p.m.–10:00 p.m.**
  Fri. and Sat.: 4:00 p.m.–11:00 p.m.
  Sun.: 1:00 p.m.–10:00 p.m.
  Open for lunch
- **CLOSING DAYS: None**
- **RESERVATIONS: Yes**
- **PARKING: Lot**
- **CREDIT CARDS: All**
- **HANDICAPPED ACCESS: Ramps; no difficulty**
- **AVERAGE CHECK FOR TWO: $20.00**

Mexican

La Placita Cafe

Plaza Palomino
2950 N. Swan Road
Tucson

881-1150

TUCSON

Here is an upscale, sophisticated Mexican restaurant that is doing things right. Preparing authentic Sonoran food fashioned "in the old style" is the specialty. The cheerful "L" shaped dining room is painted in pink and blue pastels with a bit of southwestern art on the walls. Pink tablecloths are protected by glass tops. The paper napkins are a negative.

Good, warm tortilla chips and a zesty salsa are offered soon after being seated. The menu presents a good selection of five or six different tacos, enchiladas, burros and chimichangas, plus a few combinations. These are all good and satisfying. However, our main interest is always drawn to the special dinners of fresh cabrilla cooked Hermosillo style with tomatoes, onions and chiles; chicken and beef fajitas with salsa and guacamole; the red or green chile con carnes; and the Guaymas shrimp sauteed in garlic and butter. They even have huevos rancheros over corn tortillas, and some gringo food.

The dessert list is longer than in most Mexican places and ranges from ice creams and flan to fruit chimichangas, sopapillas and almendrado. Table service is swift and efficient. The Margaritas are grande and the Mexican and American beers cold.

- **HOURS: Mon. thru Sat.: 5:00 p.m.–9:00 p.m.**
  Open for lunch
- **CLOSING DAYS: Sun.**
- **RESERVATIONS: Yes**
- **PARKING: Shopping center lot**
- **CREDIT CARDS: MC, V**
- **HANDICAPPED ACCESS: No difficulty**
- **AVERAGE CHECK FOR TWO: $20.00**

La Villa

Westin La Paloma Resort
3800 E. Sunrise Drive 577-5806
Tucson 742-6000

TUCSON

Luxury abides in this noble restaurant that is in a separate building apart from the entrance to the La Paloma resort. Dining is on two levels in several raftered rooms with a neo-colonial ambience. Arched picture windows overlook the lights of Tucson.

The menu announces an abundance of riches, principally fresh fish and seafood items. However, landlubbers are not overlooked with a very satisfying roasted duck breast with a sparkling blueberry sauce, and tasty Black Angus filet mignons — one with prawns. But this is "Tucson's restaurant for fresh fish" so enjoy crab cakes with anise sauce, yellow fin tuna with red pepper butter, mahi mahi with pineapple-macadamia butter sauce, and Coho salmon with baby shrimp and lemon grass butter sauce. The temptations go on and on. . . .

Entrees come with market-fresh vegetables and a choice of either La Villa dark lettuce salad or a cup of zesty New England clam chowder.

Do not miss the specialty meringue-ice cream-chocolate dessert called the "Desert Rose." The wine list is superb although a bit overpriced. Waiter service is not up to the standard of the cuisine.

- **HOURS: Mon. thru Sun.: 5:30–10:30 p.m.**
- **CLOSING DAYS: None**
- **RESERVATIONS: Yes**
- **PARKING: Lot and valet**
- **CREDIT CARDS: All**
- **HANDICAPPED ACCESS: No difficulty**
- **AVERAGE CHECK FOR TWO: $40.00**

Lakewood Inn

Highway 260
Lakeside 368-5153

PINETOP – LAKESIDE

This cute, picture postcard cottage on the shore of Lake of the Woods provides the beautiful setting for enjoyable dining. Two of three dining rooms with comfortable captain's chairs have large windows overlooking the tranquility of the lake with leaping fish and gliding ducks. It's difficult to imagine a more peaceful scene. This is the epitome of enjoyable dining in this area.

The bill of fare is a standard list of tempting edibles, properly prepared and attractively presented. The off-menu specials of the day have always been delightful and are strongly recommended. However, the juicy prime rib, tender steaks and seafood items all pass muster. A standout creation is the sauteed chicken breast Sonora with chiles, cheese and salsa. Another kitchen masterpiece is the Cajun shrimp.

Meals include a help-yourself family salad bowl, fresh daily vegetable, a choice of a baked potato, French fries, rice pilaf or pasta, and good, warm garlic rolls. Desserts lean toward homemade cheesecakes that seem made in heaven. The wine list covers only the basics but the prices are right. Waitress table service is generally excellent. This is a family enterprise from the front door to the kitchen and is dedicated to perfection.

- **HOURS: Mon. thru Sun.: 5:00 p.m.–10:00 p.m.**
  Open for lunch; breakfast on Fri. & Sat.
- **CLOSING DAYS: None**
- **RESERVATIONS: Yes**
- **PARKING: Lot**
- **CREDIT CARDS: MC, V**
- **HANDICAPPED ACCESS: No difficulty**
- **AVERAGE CHECK FOR TWO: $35.00**

Landmark

809 W. Main Street
Mesa 962-4652

MESA

Here is downhome cooking in the roomy, unrushed atmosphere of a restored 1906 church. The decor is spartan but enlivened by charming antiques. It's all tables and chairs, and everything is neat and clean.

The simple menu will make grandmother happy. She can enjoy old fashioned pot roast, Swiss steak, beef liver sauteed with onions, chicken fried steak, chicken livers broiled in garlic butter sauce and lightly floured fried chicken. All of these are without serious fault. Friends rave about the deviled short ribs of beef. Some 10 seafood dishes also come over well. The baked salmon or halibut with lemon butter sauce are standouts. Ditto the fried shrimp and scallops. The roast prime rib, available in two cuts, is undistinguished. Entrees come with vegetable and a choice of standard rice, baked potato, French fries or super, made-from-scratch mashed potatoes. But the very best is the salad bar.

Housed in a side room, it is probably the largest salad bar you will ever see. A visit is included with the entree price or you can solo for $7.45. Help yourself as often as you wish. Your choices of garden goodies are stupendous. Table service is efficient with fast-stepping waitresses helping where needed.

- **HOURS: Mon. thru Sat.: 4:00 p.m.–9:00 p.m.**
  Sun.: 12 noon–7:00 p.m.
  Open for lunch
- **CLOSING DAYS: None**
- **RESERVATIONS: No**
- **PARKING: Lot**
- **CREDIT CARDS: All**
- **HANDICAPPED ACCESS: Steps to second floor**
- **AVERAGE CHECK FOR TWO: $25.00**

* * * *American*

Latilla Room

The Boulders
Tom Darlington Drive 488-9020
Carefree 254-9429

CAREFREE

Nestled in the rocky desert foothills, this luxury resort complements the terrain with earthen tones, flagstone floors and regional art on walls. There are three dining rooms with panoramic views with the premier Latilla Room featuring haute cuisine of dependable excellence.

The menu is changed regularly and just about everything is superb. You take your pick from nine appetizers (ceviche, jalapeno pasta, duckling liver mousse, etc.) and some dozen main courses (poached sea bass with green chili salsa, grilled veal chop with Roquefort and lime sauce, veal, pork and lamb filets, rack of lamb, tournedos of beef, venison, etc.) There are two or three salads, which vary with the seasons. One is a simple garden salad and the other a more fascinating mixture of butter lettuce, enoki mushrooms, cherry tomatoes and other garden goodies with a super dressing.

A wide range of premises-baked pastries is offered for dessert including a chocolate, macadamia nut praline tort that won a culinary award for the chef.

There is a beautifully presented wine list with discriminating choices at appropriate prices. Waiter service has gotten more professional. Jackets are required for men.

- **HOURS: Mon. thru Sun.: 6:00 p.m.–10:00 p.m.**
  Open for lunch; brunch on Sunday
- **CLOSING DAYS: June-Sept.** • **PARKING: Lots and valet**
- **RESERVATIONS: Yes** • **CREDIT CARDS: All**
- **HANDICAPPED ACCESS: No difficulty**
- **AVERAGE CHECK FOR TWO: $65.00**

* * * *French*

L'Auberge de Sedona

301 Little Lane 282-7131
Sedona 282-1661

SEDONA

This is a small place with picture windows overlooking Oak Creek. Changed daily, the one page menu offers a deluxe six-course dinner for a prix fixe $45. You have a choice of three or four hors d'oeuvres; hot or cold soups; salad; seven or eight entrees, which includes beef, lamb, fowl and seafood dishes; dessert and beverage. Be sure to bring your appetite.

Among the hors d'oeuvres we have preferred the baked Stilton cheese with olives over the pates and terrine of seafood. The soups are always delightful whether chilled cherry with cream, Vichyssoise, or hot cream of broccoli, spinach, etc. The mimosa salad with tangy Dijon mustard never disappoints. Entrees show some exciting culinary imagination. Roast duckling is presented as seven divine slices of breast meat in brandy cream with green pepper corns. A lamb fancier should enjoy a nice innovation: grilled leg of baby lamb stuffed with spinach and Roquefort cheese. Another superb offering is pork tenderloin with red wine and black currants. All of these dishes are exquisite with potato of the day and fresh vegetable.

Desserts accent fresh fruit parfaits, tarts and cakes. A good selection of French, German and California wines is offered and there are some good prices. Table service is excellent.

- **HOURS: Mon. thru Sun.: 6:15 p.m.–10:00 p.m.**
  Open for breakfast and lunch
- **CLOSING DAYS: None**
- **RESERVATIONS: Yes**
- **PARKING: Lot**
- **CREDIT CARDS: All**
- **HANDICAPPED ACCESS: No difficulty**
- **AVERAGE CHECK FOR TWO: $90.00**

L'Ecole

Scottsdale Culinary Institute
4141 N. Scottsdale Road (Indian School)
Scottsdale 990-7639

SCOTTSDALE

Modern art and watercolors grace the walls of a single dining room with picture windows looking out over the patio-courtyard of an office building. Comfortable chairs surround attractively set tables with white linens and a small candle.

This restaurant is the showcase laboratory for the Scottsdale Culinary Institute providing guests with a selection of menu items that are always fresh and utilizing as many Arizona-grown products as possible. You enjoy food prepared by the students under the tutelage of some of Arizona's outstanding professional chefs. This is dining for the moderately adventuresome. The menu is changed weekly and may range from the pedestrian to the exotic.

Four-course meals are offered that go from appetizer through dessert. Prices range from $12 to $20 and your only additional expense is the gratuity. You usually have a choice of four each of appetizers, entrees and desserts, which may include carrot and shallot soup, red pepper mousse, baked goat cheese salad, baked Norwegian salmon with anchovy, grilled chicken with citrus, steamed fish Hunan style, ginger creme carmel, almond tarts, Baume de Venise ice cream, ad delicium. A wine is suggested for each meal. Students of the school provide table service.

- **HOURS: Wed. thru Sat.: 6:30 p.m.–9:00 p.m.**
  Open for lunch
- **CLOSING DAYS: Sun., Mon. and Tues.**
- **PARKING: Lot**
- **RESERVATIONS: Yes**
- **CREDIT CARDS: All**
- **HANDICAPPED ACCESS: No difficulty**
- **AVERAGE CHECK FOR TWO: $32.00**

* * * *Swiss*

Le Gourmand

12345 W. Indian School Road
Litchfield Park 935-1515

LITCHFIELD PARK

This is a dignified restaurant with a distinguished kitchen. The award-winning chef takes no shortcuts in his quest for culinary perfection. Thus, the easy-to-read menu is of gourmet dedication and dependable excellence. A perfect evening is assured by a European host who oversees the dining room.

The diner has two choices: order a three-course dinner which includes appetizer (or salad), entree and dessert; or order the main course only and if you wish a salad add $1.50. Your choice of appetizers includes smoked Norwegian salmon, homemade ravioli, sauteed fresh mushrooms, lobster bisque, escargots in herbed garlic butter and garden salad. They are all exquisite.

Entrees vary but will probably include ragout of rock lobster served in a puff pastry shell, fresh Norwegian salmon filets, coquille St. Jacques, sea scallops in white wine sauce with green onions, rack of lamb, beef tenderloin steak, sweetbreads, veal cordon bleu, boneless chicken sauteed with mushrooms, etc. Any one will make your hit parade. All entrees come with either potatoes of the day, buttered rice or egg noodles and/or fresh vegetables. The hot rolls are outstanding. The dessert list is sensational and includes a nice selection of cheeses. Table service is superior.

- **HOURS: Tues. thru Sun.: 5:30 p.m.–10:00 p.m.**
- **CLOSING DAYS: Mon.; July and August**
- **RESERVATIONS: Yes** • **CREDIT CARDS: All**
- **PARKING: Lot**
- **HANDICAPPED ACCESS: No difficulty**
- **AVERAGE CHECK FOR TWO: $42.00**

* * *French*

Le Rendez-Vous

3844 E. Fort Lowell Road (Alvernon)
Tucson 323-7373

The warm, intimate atmosphere of a small French bistro beckons you enter. Cozy tables are set with decorative china, red tablecloths, candles and fresh flowers. The formally-attired waiters are adept and provide good service. Piped-in music is pleasant.

The offerings are not extensive, but all will tantalize. There are three soups (try the cream of summer squash) and four salads. We recommend the Le Rendez-Vous salade with spinach, red-leaf lettuce, fresh vegetables and a wonderfully seasoned house dressing.

Entree enticements range from chicken breast baked in brown sauce with sherry, to a zippy pepper steak, to veal in cream sauce with apples and French brandy (wondrous). Dumplings stuffed with mousse of fish, lobster in champagne sauce and poached salmon top the list of gourmet sea fare. Our personal favorite is the cote de boeuf grille aux herbes; prime rib of beef for two that is perfectly prepared with an au jus that is incomparable.

Meals include potato and vegetable warmed tableside with your entree. Dessert selections are modest but memorable — the Gran Marnier souffle is a standout and the chocolate meringue cake is a must for all chocolate fiends! The wine list is impeccably presented and includes moderate to expensive wines from worldwide vineyards.

- **HOURS: Tues. thru Sun.: 6:00 p.m.–10:00 p.m.**
- **CLOSING DAYS: Mon.**
- **RESERVATIONS: Yes**
- **PARKING: Lot**
- **CREDIT CARDS: All**
- **HANDICAPPED ACCESS: No difficulty**
- **AVERAGE CHECK FOR TWO: $45.00**

* * *

Continental
Swiss

Le Rhone

Plaza del Rio Center
9401 W. Thunderbird Road
Peoria 933-0151

PEORIA

This Sun City restaurant is a gastronomic marriage made in heaven. The friendly pleasant atmosphere is conducive to quiet dining enjoyment. Comfortable arm chairs encourage a leisurely evening. The piano music is relaxing. In total, a restaurant that is a real charmer. This is the best eating in Sun City.

The fascinating menu offers complete three-course dinners: appetizer, entree and dessert. For appetizers you choose perhaps from a divine tartelette of three mushrooms, poached salmon mousse, galantine of duck, soups or a perfect Le Rhone salad. For entrees your cup runneth over: boneless chicken breast a l'Indienne with creamy curry sauce, almonds and chutney, poached Nova Scotia sea scallops with Hollandaise, three versions of Dover sole, small lobster tails in white wine sauce, veal sweetbreads, beef stroganoff, a rib rack of spring lamb, beef tenderloin, venison medallions, chateaubriand, etc. Some dozen desserts include all manner of cakes, sundaes, mousses, etc. Seconds are offered on vegetables, potatoes and rice.

Warm dinner rolls are excellent, and a thoughtful selection of reasonably priced house wines is offered. Table service is brisk and efficient.

- **HOURS: Tues. thru Sun.: 5:30 p.m.–10:00 p.m.**
  Open for lunch on Wednesday only
- **CLOSING DAYS: Mons.**
- **RESERVATIONS: Yes**
- **PARKING: Lot**
- **CREDIT CARDS: All**
- **HANDICAPPED ACCESS: Ramps where needed**
- **AVERAGE CHECK FOR TWO: $40.00**

Lone Star

6003 N. 16th Street, Phoenix 248-7827
7000 E. Shea Blvd., Scottsdale 443-3777

PHOENIX – SCOTTSDALE

Believe it or not, there is a little bit of Texas in Phoenix. Considered by many to be the best little steakhouse in Arizona, this is eating "Texas Style" with loud music, neon beer signs, and walls plastered with old auto license tags, soft drink ads and a collection of peaked caps. On Formica topped tables in booths the bottles of A-1 sauce, tabasco, mustard, ketchup and chile peppers are all within easy reach.

The limited blackboard menu has eight steaks, chicken ka-bob, one shrimp item and a bowl of chili. The most popular steaks are probably the 12-oz. rib eye or Freidy's 8-oz. filet (that's not a misspelling). Bigger appetites can go for the 18-oz. T-bone and the 22-oz. Lone Star. Every Thursday they have a smoked prime rib special, which is marvelous. All steaks come with great buttermilk biscuits, an above average lettuce salad and choice of mashed potatoes with country gravy or baked potatoes sliced and roasted.

Do not miss the bread pudding with whisky sauce. It is divine. They often have a good strawberry shortcake. Table service is fast and furious, the beer is cold, but auto parking on 16th St. can be rough.

- **HOURS: Mon. thru Thurs.: 5:00 p.m.–10:00 p.m.**
  Fri. and Sat.: 5:00 p.m.–11:00 p.m.
  Sun.: 4:00 p.m.–10:00 p.m.
  Open for lunch
- **CLOSING DAYS: None**
- **RESERVATIONS: Yes**
- **PARKING: Lots**
- **CREDIT CARDS: All**
- **HANDICAPPED ACCESS: No difficulty**
- **AVERAGE CHECK FOR TWO: $28.00**

Luby's Cafeterias

A total of eight convenient locations in the Valley of the Sun and two in Tucson. Consult your telephone directory for addresses.

PHX – MESA – SCTSDL – CHANDLER – TUCSON

This is a self-serve Texas chain that has the largest selection of salads, entrees and desserts of any of Arizona's many cafeterias. These neat, well-lit places are cheerful and inviting. Taped music adds to the pleasant atmosphere. For the money they cannot be beat.

There are at least 15 entrees that will range from salmon croquettes and chopped sirloin steak to sweet and sour pork chops, roast beef and chicken liver with onions. There is no lack of choice among vegetables and potatoes with at least 14 that are either steamed, boiled, baked or sauteed. The salad selection is a rabbit's heaven. You can go for the standard lettuce salad, and spinach salad with egg and bacon dressing to Spanish slaw with red peppers and pickle slices, carrot and raisin salad, ad infinitum.

You also choose from two soups of the day, of which the seafood gumbo is a winner with us. There is a nice selection of breads, biscuits, rolls and muffins. Desserts include all manner of fresh baked fruit, cream and icebox pies, cakes puddings and more. They are remarkably delicious. Hot tea, coffee and iced tea are replenished at your table at no extra charge. Cleanup service is fast by smiling, enthusiastic waitresses. No alcoholic drinks are available.

- **HOURS: Mon. thru Sun.: 10:45 a.m.–8:00 p.m.**
- **CLOSING DAYS: None**
- **RESERVATIONS: No**
- **PARKING: Lots**
- **CREDIT CARDS: None**
- **HANDICAPPED ACCESS: No difficulty**
- **AVERAGE CHECK FOR TWO: $13.00**

* *

Thai
Japanese

Malee Chu's

The Borgata
6166 N. Scottsdale Road
Scottsdale

948-8012

SCOTTSDALE

This is the most elegant of all Thai restaurants in Arizona, and is in harmony with the sauve sophistication of The Borgata. And the cuisine is worth a pilgrimage! You are seated in black and white cool comfort at booths or tables in one of two dining rooms. A Japanese sushi-sashimi bar is at one end.

The menu promises a multitude of dream foods —and delivers. For the timid, spicy dishes are so marked. The specialty dishes are all standouts and no MSG is used. Try the wonderful Evil Princess with chicken, lemon grass, coconut milk and spices. Either of two roast duck dishes, one with curry and the other with spinach, are heavenly. The Siamese chicken, Malee blackened N.Y. steak Thai-style, and Bangkok steamed fish are all exciting and memorable. If you enjoy curried foods, do not miss the Gaeng Ped, a red curry with beef or chicken, bamboo shoots, sweet peas and carrots in coconut sauce. Praised by friends are the spicy sauteed cashew nuts and vegetables with choice of chicken, beef or pork. The list of delectable delights goes on and on. Table service is swift and efficient.

- **HOURS: Mon. thru Sun.: 5:30 p.m.–10:00 p.m.**
  Open for lunch
- **CLOSING DAYS: None**
- **RESERVATIONS: Yes**
- **PARKING: Lot**
- **CREDIT CARDS: All**
- **HANDICAPPED ACCESS: No difficulty; steps to sushi bar**
- **AVERAGE CHECK FOR TWO: $25.00**

Malee's on Main

7131 E. Main Street
Scottsdale

994-3474
947-6042

SCOTTSDALE

Enjoy a gourmet dinner in exotic Thailand in a smallish place with a cute bar in the corner. Attractive floral china grace tables covered with green and peach tablecloths. A mini outdoor patio offers dining al fresco.

The sparkling menu covers a good range of tasty Thai cuisine, and you can order your dishes mild, medium or spicy hot. In general the portions are not large, so plan on ordering three dishes with rice for two people. There are eight exotic salads, six exciting soups, seven spicy curry dishes, three tempting plates for vegetable lovers, and a nice list of specialty entrees with beef, chicken, pork or fish. Disappointments are rare but exciting taste sensations common. This is your chance to be adventuresome.

Do not miss the combination appetizer with delicious spring rolls, beef satay, Thai toast, won tons, mee krob rice noodles and three sauces. Another must is beef or chicken Panang with mild curry, spicy coconut sauce and mint leaves. Shrimp dishes all come over well including a sensational grilled shrimp salad and shrimp in a clay pot. The pork entrees have always been juicy and memorable. The Thai custard dessert made of coconut cream instead of milk is a perfect finish. Table service is erratic.

- **HOURS:** **Mon. thru Sat.: 5:00 p.m.–9:30 p.m.**
  Open for lunch
- **CLOSING DAYS: Sun.**
- **RESERVATIONS: Yes**
- **PARKING: Street**
- **CREDIT CARDS: All**
- **HANDICAPPED ACCESS: No difficulty**
- **AVERAGE CHECK FOR TWO: $30.00**

* * * *Continental Italian*

Mancuso's

The Borgata
6166 N. Scottsdale Road (Lincoln)
Scottsdale 948-9988

SCOTTSDALE

In keeping with The Borgata surroundings, Mancuso's offers exquisite food in an Italian Renaissance castle atmosphere. With a high beamed ceiling and imaginative use of mirrors for spaciousness, this striking setting will live in memory as will the culinary artistry of the chef.

The extensive menu abounds in classical northern Italian and continental dishes prepared with finesse. A couple of off-menu items add excitement. The double French lamb chops, filet of sole or chicken Oscar with crabmeat, asparagus and bearnaise sauce, and the tournedos Henri IV with bearnaise sauce and stuffed mushrooms are standout dishes. Other delights include fettucine with shrimp and scallops, and duckling with a choice of two sauces: orange or raspberry.

With entrees the diner receives soup of the day, a nice mixed green lettuce salad with a piquant creamy Italian dressing, a refreshing sherbet palate cleanser, and a pasta accompaniment. Desserts are displayed on a tray and are rich and memorable.

Table service by black-tied waiters is usually smooth and professionally competent. The wine list at Mancuso's reflects the ambience of this outstanding restaurant: first class all the way.

- **HOURS: Mon. thru Sun.: 5:30 p.m.–10:30 p.m.**
  Open for lunch
- **CLOSING DAYS: None**
- **RESERVATIONS: Yes**
- **PARKING: Lot and valet**
- **CREDIT CARDS: All**
- **HANDICAPPED ACCESS: No difficulty**
- **AVERAGE CHECK FOR TWO: $45.00**

Mandarin Delight
5309 N. 7th Street, Phoenix 274-5204

Ming's
3300 S. Mill Avenue, Tempe 966-6464

Wok & Roll
3741 E. Thomas Road, Phoenix 267-1171

PHOENIX – TEMPE

These delightful oriental oases continue to be a happy joy for restaurant goers. Mandarin and spicy Szechuan dishes are served in an atmosphere appropriate to an epicurean experience.

These are the only restaurants in the Valley that serve Peking duck without several days' notice. This specialty is of classic elegance, and if you have not savored this delicately seasoned dish, here is your chance. Besides the Peking duck they also specialize in other duck dishes that are no less impressive. However, do try the diced chicken with walnuts and plum sauce that is a gastronomic delight, as is the lemon chicken. The shrimp with ginger sauce, and the sizzling filet of beef and scallops also deserve raves. Ditto the Yu Shang scallops with water chestnuts, mushrooms and baby corn.

Cocktails, wine and beer are served. Family owned and operated, attentive table service is usually assured.

- **HOURS:** Mon. thru Thurs.: 5:00 p.m.–10:00 p.m.
  Fri. and Sat.: 5:00 p.m.–11:00 p.m.
  Sun.: 12 noon–10:00 p.m.
  Open for lunch except at Ming's
- **CLOSING DAYS:** None
- **RESERVATIONS:** Yes
- **PARKING:** Lots
- **CREDIT CARDS:** All
- **HANDICAPPED ACCESS:** No difficulty
- **AVERAGE CHECK FOR TWO:** $18.00

Mangia Bene

La Posada Plaza
4949 E. Lincoln Drive (Tatum)
Paradise Valley 840-8670

PARADISE VALLEY

Here is quality Italian cooking in a casual yet upbeat atmosphere of the charming Red Lion La Posada Resort. Best of all the prices are modest and you will not go away hungry. Dining is at tables and banquettes in a series of white painted, slumpblock walled rooms with soft carpeting. A creative piano player plays happy tunes during the evening. A comfortable bar area invites lingering.

The menu ranges from a long list of skillfully prepared pastas, priced from $8.95 to $9.95, three pizzas, four veal and five chicken dishes to various other temptations such as an inviting eggplant with smooth ricotta cheese and marinara sauce, stuffed rolled beef braciola, tender baby calves liver with onions and pancetta, etc. We and our friends have basically found everything above criticism.

With each entree you receive an unlimited, help-yourself garden salad mixture brought to your table in a large bowl. You also receive constant refills of warm, savory Italian focaccia bread. The modest wine list is limited to California and Italian labels but prices are very fair. The dessert tray accents rich, smooth cheesecakes — all of which are heartstoppers. Table service by watchful waiters and waitresses brings no complaint. Mangia Bene is an unrecognized bargain in a high rent district.

- **HOURS: Mon. thru Sun.: 5:00 p.m.–10:00 p.m.**
- **CLOSING DAYS: None**
- **RESERVATIONS: Yes**
- **PARKING: Lot**
- **CREDIT CARDS: All**
- **HANDICAPPED ACCESS: Low steps in outside patio**
- **AVERAGE CHECK FOR TWO: $26.00**

Marilyn's 1st Mexican

12631 N. Tatum Boulevard (Cactus)
Phoenix 953-2121

A cute, cozy and congenial little place in peach and blue with piped-in Mexican music, good food and fast service. There are booths and tables, lots of blonde wood and a hustle-bustle that confirms its popularity.

The menu ranges the spectrum of Mexican cooking. While it does not soar to gastronomic heights neither does it wallow in mediocrity. In short, good solid food at reasonable prices and few disappointments. The taco chips at the beginning are warm and crisp, and are replenished regularly at no charge. The two accompanying sauces are appropriately zingy. Ice tea comes in a demi-carafe — the equivalent of more than two glasses.

The following are menu standouts: the sizzling chicken and beef fajitas, the beef burros, the special beef chimichangas, the pollo fundido in the flour tortilla covered with cheese, and the cheese quesadillas with that great spicy guacamole on the side. The chili relleno con carne also deserves a rave as does the Mexican pizza for one or two. They recently added a great fajitadilla, which is a quesadilla filled with fajita steak or chicken with peppers, onions and tomatoes.

The Margaritas are good and the sangria has character. Table service is fast and furious by waitresses in colorful native costumes.

- **HOURS:** Mon. thru Sun.: 5:00 p.m.–10:00 p.m.
  Open for lunch
- **CLOSING DAYS:** None
- **RESERVATIONS:** No
- **PARKING:** Shopping center lot
- **CREDIT CARDS:** All
- **HANDICAPPED ACCESS:** No difficulty
- **AVERAGE CHECK FOR TWO:** $18.00

* * * *Catalan*

Marquesa

Scottsdale Princess Resort
7575 E. Princess Drive
Scottsdale 585-4848

SCOTTSDALE

The premier dining room at Scottsdale's newest posh resort is a dignified, comfortable and formal place. Large jars of pickled fruits and vegetables are real conversation pieces, while the pink and beige walls add a warm glow to the room. This is luxury dining par excellence in an elegant atmosphere of Old World charm.

Olive oil-based Catalan cuisine is Spanish food like you have never had before. Evian water is poured and your repast begins with pan boli, a crisp-crusted bread topped with tomato and olive oil. As an appetizer grilled breast of duck with Port wine and figs may appeal, or perhaps sauteed sweetbreads with mushrooms and shallots. A fresh and pretty salad comes with the meal and you have a choice of tarragon or raspberry vinaigrette dressings. Praiseworthy entrees of epicurean status include braised rabbit with a peppery tomato sauce, shrimp sauteed in almond cream, breast of chicken in crystallized pear sauce, and a fabulous paella Valenciana with pork, veal and game.

The dessert trolley is breath-taking. The wine list is sophisticated and obviously prepared with great care by a dedicated oenophile. Servers in white with colorful berets and sashes provide exemplary service.

- **HOURS: Mon. thru Sun.: 6:00 p.m.–11:00 p.m.**
  Open for lunch; brunch on Sunday
- **CLOSING DAYS: Mid-June to October**
- **RESERVATIONS: Yes**
- **PARKING: Hotel lot and valet** • **CREDIT CARDS All**
- **HANDICAPPED ACCESS: No difficulty**
- **AVERAGE CHECK FOR TWO $70.00**

Mary Elaine's

Phoenician Resort
6000 E. Camelback Road
Phoenix 941-8200

PHOENIX

This handsome, two level dining room exemplifies both the glitz and glamour of this luxurious resort at the foot of Camelback Mountain. High on the fifth floor the lights of Scottsdale twinkle through large picture windows onto creamy marble pillars and steps, perfectly set tables, fresh flowers and candles. Mirrors accent the beauty and serenity of the scene.

The a la carte menu reads like a fantasy of riches, and most come over well. Daily selections of the chef are listed on a small insert on the first page of the menu. These have always been tops and are highly recommended. Sadly, many dishes on the menu, which is changed regularly, lack pizazz. The rack of lamb with herbs, the sauteed veal medallions with eggplant and tomatoes, the roasted baby chicken with rosemary, lemon and sundried tomatoes are all noble efforts but have no sparkle. However, the steaks and fresh fish creations bring no complaint. The corn soup and the four salads are wonderful to taste and behold.

The dinner rolls that accompany the meals are bakery fresh. The desserts are fantastic. The wine list is an extensive mix of international vintages and your bottle is served in a silver sea shell. A well trained staff provides top notch table service.

- **HOURS: Mon. thru Sat.: 6:00 p.m.–10:30 p.m.**
- **CLOSING DAYS: Sun.; Mon. & Tues. during summer**
- **PARKING: Garage and valet** • **RESERVATIONS: Yes**
- **CREDIT CARDS: All**
- **HANDICAPPED ACCESS: Elevator to 5th floor**
- **AVERAGE CHECK FOR TWO: $80.00**

Milano's

1044 E. Camelback Road
Phoenix 241-1044

PHOENIX

A quaint old home has been transformed into a fine dining establishment with a warm, inviting atmosphere. The beveled glass and inlaid wood entrance door suggests an older more tranquil period and sets the tone for the evening. Gentling Italian music adds to the mood. Bustling activity in a cozy bar area does not intrude.

Kitchen artistry is best seen in the five chicken and five veal dishes that make lavish use of fine Italian cheeses, fresh herbs and Italian sauces. Bowing to a declining culinary trend they also prepare an excellent blackened red snapper that can be peppered either hot or mild. Other seafood dishes accent shrimp. The eight pasta dishes come over well and the kitchen-prepared Caesar salad is zippy and enjoyable. There are always two or three specials of the day that are usually worth considering.

All entrees come with a good daily fresh soup or an above average garden green salad with the house Italian dressing. The wine list has limited range but the prices will please. An attractive dessert tray of calorie laden pastries is presented for your review by the waitress. Table service is savvy and attentive.

- **HOURS: Mon. thru Sat.: 5:00 p.m.–11:00 p.m.**
  Open for lunch
- **CLOSING DAYS: Sun.**
- **RESERVATIONS: Yes**
- **PARKING: Lot**
- **CREDIT CARDS: All**
- **HANDICAPPED ACCESS: No difficulty**
- **AVERAGE CHECK FOR TWO: $38.00**

Mining Camp

Apache Trail — 4 Miles north of
Apache Junction 982-3181

APACHE JUNCTION

At the base of Superstition Mountain, here is a replica of a mining camp cook shanty with hearty western grub served on long, wood tables on planked floors. Wooden benches and stainless steel "tin" plates and cups take the diner back to the old days of pioneer Arizona. However, no alcoholic drinks are served.

The restaurant is a rough-hewn Ponderosa pine structure that will serve several hundred at a sitting and is surrounded by rustic buildings. It's a little noisy, but the kids will love it.

There are always platters of golden brown roast chicken with dressing, slices of roast sirloin of beef, and barbecued beef ribs. You can also have delightfully prepared prime ribs of beef or a tender 10 or 12 oz. charbroiled rib eye steak, but there are no seconds on these.

A delicious cole slaw is served family-style, along with tasty, oven-hot baked beans. There are sourdough rolls, homemade raisin bread with tub butter, and a homemade fruit jam with a jigger or two of rum added. The coffee comes to the table in large coffee pots on a help-yourself basis and the meal is complete with some nice crunchy chocolate chip cookies. A 10% discount is available to senior citizens.

- **HOURS: Tues. thru Sat.: 4:00 p.m.–9:30 p.m.**
  Sun.: 12 noon–9:30 p.m.
- **CLOSING DAYS: Mondays**
- **RESERVATIONS: Yes**
- **PARKING: Lot**
- **CREDIT CARDS: MC, V**
- **HANDICAPPED ACCESS: Four steps at entrance**
- **AVERAGE CHECK FOR TWO: $25.00**

Molly Butler Lodge

Greer 735-7226

GREER

On the edge of the enchanted White Mountains, Arizona's oldest guest lodge has been accommodating hungry travelers since 1910. The shingled wooden building overlooks lush valley meadows surrounded by hills and mountains. Deer abound in the area. It's difficult to imagine a prettier spot.

There are two connecting dining rooms next to a comfortable lounge with a stone fireplace. Beautiful antique chairs and tables, some round and some square, are nicely spaced. The menu is modest with only 14 entrees and two dessert selections. The specialty, and sure to please, is roast prime rib au jus with creamed horseradish. There are three tender, juicy cuts from $12 to $16. The Molly Butler special steak is another strong recommendation. It is a lean top sirloin, smothered in rich, creamy country-style Mormon gravy. We recommend you request the gravy on the side because it is very rich and includes ground sirloin for taste and body. People have boasted to us about the Hot Dang Chili, Georgia fried chicken, trout almondine and the fried shrimp.

All dinners include your choice of a good homemade soup or average salad, choice of baked potato, mountain rice or French fries, and excellent fresh baked bread. The fresh baked pies are the dessert standouts. A rustic cocktail lounge and bar adjoin the dining room.

- **HOURS: Sun. thru Thurs.: 5:00 p.m.–9:00 p.m.**
Fri. and Sat.: 5:00 p.m.–10:00 p.m.
- **CLOSING DAYS: None**
- **RESERVATIONS: Yes**
- **PARKING: Lot**
- **CREDIT CARDS: MC, V**
- **HANDICAPPED ACCESS: Flight of 12 steps**
- **AVERAGE CHECK FOR TWO: $32.00**

Mr. C's

4302 N. Scottsdale Road (6th Avenue)
Scottsdale 941-4460

SCOTTSDALE

Arizona has long awaited an upscale, distinguished Chinese restaurant that is quiet and elegant, with polished table service, an imaginative menu and culinary artistry. Thus Mr. C's is a welcome newcomer to our galaxy of fine dining rooms. Enjoy a repast fit for a mandarin in oriental opulence.

If you crave a standard dinner as served in most Chinese restaurants, forget Mr. C's. You will not find chop suey, chow mein, sweet and sour shrimp, etc. on the menu. But you will find gunpowder lobster, firecracker beef and prawns each served with the chef's special chili sauce; macadamia and pecan chicken and four ready-to-order Peking duck dishes. Also available are shark fin soup and appetizers of minced pork dumplings and minced quail with pine nuts, mushrooms and red peppers. This is the place for the Chinese food connoisseur.

In addition to the superior cuisine, all dishes are presented on silver plates and you dine off fine Morning Glory china. A special coffee blend is brewed at your table. Wine is kept cool in silver buckets. And you enjoy your repast amidst beautiful Chinese ceramics, paintings and artworks imported from Taiwan and Hong Kong. A full line of cocktails is available.

- **HOURS: Sun. thru Thurs.: 5:00 p.m.–10:00 p.m.**
  Fri. and Sat.: 5:00 p.m.–11:00 p.m.
  Open for lunch
- **CLOSING DAYS: None**
- **RESERVATIONS: Yes**
- **PARKING: Street**
- **CREDIT CARDS: All**
- **HANDICAPPED ACCESS: No difficulty**
- **AVERAGE CHECK FOR TWO: $35.00**

* * * *American*

Mr. Louie's

645 E. Missouri Avenue
Phoenix 263-8000

PHOENIX

One of the Valley's most personable restaurateurs oversees a class act in a semi-formal, picture-windowed room overlooking bubbling water fountains and street bustle. But no noise intrudes to detract from a beautiful dining experience. Good spacing of tables and comfortable booths assure privacy; green plants and Norman Rockwell lithographs dignify the decor.

The contemporary menu reflects Mr. Louie's classic adherence to quality and tradition. The ragout of escargot appetizer and the cream of broccoli soup are great starters. Entree treasures include roasted duck breast with peach sauce, expertly cooked sweetbreads in a cream sauce, royal Mandarin sea scallops and a perfect prime rib of beef au jus. The off-menu daily fresh fish has always been enjoyable, but the rack of lamb and pan roasted game hen are rather mundane. There is also a modest Heart Smart menu, recommended by the American Heart Association, that includes grilled halibut, filet mignon and lean N.Y. steak.

All dinners come with soup or salad, a choice of two divine dressings, an aromatic bleu cheese or the specialty honey yogurt, vegetable, and potato of the day or rice. The dessert tray is lavish; the wine list sound. A finely honed, disciplined staff is perfect.

- **HOURS: Mon. thru Sun.: 5:00 p.m.–10:30 p.m.**
  Open for lunch
- **CLOSING DAYS: None**
- **RESERVATIONS: Yes**
- **PARKING: Garage and valet**
- **CREDIT CARDS: All**
- **HANDICAPPED ACCESS: No difficulty**
- **AVERAGE CHECK FOR TWO: $40.00**

Murphy's

201 N. Cortez
Prescott 445-4044

PRESCOTT

Nostalgic dining in an old mercantile store built in 1890 and listed in the National Historic Register. Old photos and antiques abound. Grey walls and a high ceiling are beautified with green plants, Burgundy accents and stained wood booths.

A blackboard above the hostess' desk lists daily fresh fish offerings: sea bass, black tipped shark, king salmon, Hawaiian kajiki, etc. The menu at the tables expands the repertoire. Thus, you can enjoy an intriguing seafood gumbo of shrimp, scallops and whitefish or a nice seafood brochette of the above items spaced with onions and peppers. Although untested by us, they also offer shrimp, scallop and lobster brochettes, steamed king crab legs and lobster tails.

Landlubbers are not forsaken. We have received excellent reports on the four cuts of roast prime rib of beef and top sirloin steak. A special treat and enjoyable is the pollo de Pablo, a half tender chicken marinated in fruit juices and herbs, and broiled over mesquite. Can't decide between seafood, beef or chicken? They will combine any two for your dining enjoyment and price the combo accordingly. All entrees include soup or fresh garden salad, on-premises baked bread and choice of rice Pilaf, new boiled potatoes or house fries.

- **HOURS: Mon. thru Sun.: 4:30 p.m.–11:00 p.m.**
  Open for lunch
- **CLOSING DAYS: None**
- **RESERVATIONS: Yes**
- **PARKING: Street**
- **CREDIT CARDS: All**
- **HANDICAPPED ACCESS: No difficulty**
- **AVERAGE CHECK FOR TWO: $26.00**

Nineteen Twelve

Sheraton San Marcos
San Marcos Place
Chandler 963-6655

This dining room is named for the year 1912 when Arizona gained statehood and construction began on the state's first public resort — the San Marcos. The smallish, two-tiered dining room reflects the casual elegance and relaxed pace of that time, and the draped windows, and rattan seating exemplify the furnishings of 1912 with a scene that conveys comfort and intimacy.

The classical bill of fare has been contemporized with modern preparation and artistic, enticing presentations. Your choice is limited to five appetizers, six soups and salads and ten entrees. Each entree includes potato and vegetable of the day. All salads are a la carte.

A standout appetizer is the blackened prawns and escargots in a pastry shell. The Princess salad is wondrous with hearts of palm and artichokes, endive, radicchio, etc. Choice entrees are the Navajo rack of lamb with pine nut crust, the free range venison medallions with prickly pear sauce, and the Sonoran soft shell crabs in blue corn meal with papaya salsa.

The extensive wine list has some superior labels at acceptable prices. Desserts are fresh fruits with liqueurs and cremes, and a selection of sinful pastries. Service by formally dressed waiters is impeccable.

- **HOURS: Tues. thru Sat.: 6:00 p.m.–9:30 p.m.**
- **CLOSING DAYS: Sun. & Mon., other days in summer**
- **RESERVATIONS: Yes** • **CREDIT CARDS: All**
- **PARKING: Hotel parking lot and street**
- **HANDICAPPED ACCESS: No difficulty**
- **AVERAGE CHECK FOR TWO: $60.00**

Oak Creek Owl

329 Highway 179
Sedona 282-3532

SEDONA

After 32 years the "Owl" continues as one of Sedona's favorite gourmet restaurants. As always, it is cozy and comfortable with the walls covered with interesting owl art. An expanded deck has bar service and tables for outside dining — weather permitting.

The menu is probably the most extensive in northern Arizona. The rack of veal glazed with herbs and Dijon mustard, and the roast Long Island ducking are old favorites. Recently added to the menu is an outstanding grilled pork tenderloin, scallop of veal Marsala, N.Y. pepper steak, and Louisiana seafood gumbo and chicken Parmesan. The standing rib roast au jus is as good as ever. If you like soups, the locals say these are the best in northern Arizona.

With your gourmet meal you receive a fresh specialty soup *and* salad, both of which are excellent. The green lettuce salad includes crunchy almonds, as well as raw mushrooms, bean sprouts, tomatoes and croutons. Both the honey-French and sesame-vinaigrette dressings are superior.

Waiter service is attentive and professional. The wine list is the best in Sedona with the house wine being exceptional. The cheesecakes and raspberry Bavarian pie are great desserts.

- **HOURS:** **Mon. thru Sun.: 5:00 p.m.–11:00 p.m.**
  Open for lunch
- **CLOSING DAYS: None**
- **CREDIT CARDS: MC, V**
- **PARKING: Lot and valet**
- **RESERVATIONS: Yes**
- **HANDICAPPED ACCESS: Ramps where needed**
- **AVERAGE CHECK FOR TWO: $42.00**

Oaxaca

Pinnacle Peak Village Plaza
8711 E. Pinnacle Peak Road (Pima Road)
Scottsdale 998-2222

SCOTTSDALE

Fine dining can be enjoyed on the second floor above an old Spanish colonial courtyard overlooking the twinkling lights of Scottsdale. Seated at tables with heavy, straightback chairs, a bit uncomfortable, you enjoy the desert scenery and a diverse bill of fare. Weather permitting there is outdoor balcony dining.

Menu highlights that we can attest to include an excellent Southwestern chicken topped with Jack cheese and jalapeno peppers with avocado, pork loin, the tender, juicy prime rib of beef available in two cuts, both the petit and regular filet mignon; and the half duck BBQ roasted and topped with Sonoran barbeque sauce. The baby back ribs are good but not memorable, and the teriyaki chicken does not excite. The fresh fish items (salmon, swordfish, etc.) satisfy.

The bland green lettuce salad is a disappointment although the creamy ranch and Italian dressings are great. Fresh, crunchy vegetables accompany all entrees and the twice-baked potato with cheese is a real high spot. A nice warm assortment of bakery-fresh rolls and butter complement the dinner. The Oaxaca mud pie with whipped cream is sinfully rich. Service by fast-stepping waiters and waitresses is excellent. The wine list is extensive and prices are right.

- **HOURS: Mon. thru Sun.: 5:30 p.m.–10:00 p.m.**
- **CLOSING DAYS: None**
- **RESERVATIONS: Yes**
- **PARKING: Lot**
- **CREDIT CARDS: All**
- **HANDICAPPED ACCESS: Use elevator**
- **AVERAGE CHECK FOR TWO: $40.00**

Orangerie

Arizona Biltmore Resort
24th Street and Missouri Avenue
Phoenix 954-2507

PHOENIX

The finest cuisine is served with elegance and style amid the cascading luminescence of crystal chandeliers, garden greenery, picture windows and soft opulence. This is expensive dining, but as Emilio Gucci says, "quality is remembered long after price is forgotten."

The award-winning menu is changed seasonally. Salads range from warm asparagus with red oak lettuce to imaginative arrangements of raddichio and mache with creative dressings. Pieces de resistance are undoubtedly the lobster tempura, Korean chili seared sea scallops, medallions of black buck antelope, roast Chinese crispy duck, veal T-bone steak, and sauteed medallions of capon, lamb and veal with garlic-chive sabayon. There are also a couple of steaks, pan-seared Chinook salmon and halibut. The abundance of gastronomic delights is overpowering. Decision making is not easy.

With every entree there are picture-perfect fresh vegetables and other garnishments. Spoil yourself with the chocolate mousse or a selection of fresh baked tarts and pastries from the dessert cart. There are also some great souffles. Attentive, professional waiter service is a hallmark and rarely falters. The wine presentation is one of the best in the valley.

- **HOURS: Mon. thru Sun.: 6:00 p.m.–11:00 p.m.**
  Open for lunch
- **CLOSING DAYS: Sun. thru Tues. during summer**
- **RESERVATIONS: Yes** • **CREDIT CARDS: All**
- **PARKING: Lots and valet**
- **HANDICAPPED ACCESS: Ramps where needed**
- **AVERAGE CHECK FOR TWO: $63.00**

Oscar Taylor

Biltmore Fashion Park
2420 E. Camelback Road 956-5705
Phoenix 954-6063

Decor in this popular place is 1923 Chicago nostalgia and reminds us of the Berghof in the Windy City. A political poster of Richard Daly overlooking the dessert display sets the tone. In his hey-day Mayor Daly could always deliver the votes. Regrettably Oscar Taylor cannot always deliver on the quality of food it serves.

It's booths and tables, no tablecloths, ceiling fans, old fashioned globed chandeliers, brick and stone walls, and wood partitions. The menu is old time stressing tasty beef, BBQ ribs, veal and fresh seafood. There are three good steaks plus filet Wellington, and the prime N.Y. au poivre with cognac Dijon sauce is the most exciting. The prime rib is acceptable. The chef has a fine touch with veal and the mesquite grilled veal rib chop stuffed with spinach and prosciutto ham is excellent. The daily fresh seafood choices are always good. The zucchini muffins, cheese, and raisin rolls are great and vary day to day.

The dinner salad, curly French fries, cole slaw, and creamed spinach are outstanding. Desserts made on the premises are good, the portions large, but are cloyingly sweet. Table service conveys warmth and sincerity. A bargain menu is offered from 5:00 to 6:30 p.m.

- **HOURS: Sun. thru Thurs.: 5:00 p.m.–10:00 p.m.**
  Fri. and Sat.: 5:00 p.m.–11:00 p.m.
  Open for lunch
- **CLOSING DAYS: Holidays**
- **RESERVATIONS: Yes**
- **PARKING: Lot**
- **CREDIT CARDS: All**
- **HANDICAPPED ACCESS: No difficulty**
- **AVERAGE CHECK FOR TWO: $46.00**

The Other Place

A total of four convenient locations in the Valley of the Sun and one in Tucson. Consult your telephone directory for addresses.

PHOENIX – SCTSDL – TEMPE – MESA – TUCSON

These are popular eating places owned and managed by Dale Anderson, one of Arizona's most well known and peripatetic restaurateurs. The food is basic American fare, nothing daring or innovative but satisfying and filling. The adobe-style Scottsdale restaurant on Lincoln Drive is the most popular and probably the best. Some of the others are in hotels and motels and suffer accordingly.

The limited menu is pinned to a corkboard and waiters will announce daily specials. Enjoy a superb gazpacho or soup of the day, which has always been delicious. The cheddar cheese, broccoli and beef barley soups are great. You mix your salad at your table from a large bowl of crisp greens and other veggies. Four dressings are also brought to your table.

During our various visits, we have thoroughly enjoyed the veal Oscar, the prime rib and the fresh fish items. The skillet full of fried chicken with hot biscuits and honey rates a special rave. The beef kabob has been disappointing. However, the lobster tail is one of the best in the Valley.

The hot breads and the choices on the dessert tray are good. Table service can be very erratic.

- **HOURS: Sun. thru Thurs.: 5:00 p.m.–11:00 p.m.**
  Fri. and Sat.: 5:00 p.m.–12 midnight
  Open for lunch; brunch on Sun.
- **CLOSING DAYS: None**
- **RESERVATIONS: Yes**
- **PARKING: Lots and valet**
- **CREDIT CARDS: All**
- **HANDICAPPED ACCESS: No difficulty**
- **AVERAGE CHECK FOR TWO: $35.00**

The Outback

Hwy. 80 – 6 miles west of
Bisbee 432-2333

BISBEE

Don't let the outside appearance fool you. Here is gracious dining in a country atmosphere in the Mule Mountains. The interior is full of antiques for sale and decor. Ask for a porch table overlooking the river vegetation. Taped music is pleasant.

You will find no surprises on the menu, just good food, properly prepared and served in nostalgic surroundings. There are two cuts of prime rib and N.Y. steak, which are also available in combination with lobster or crablegs. All come over well. We also like the lazy lobster casserole with mushrooms, shallots, white wine, etc. If you like poultry, try the breast of chicken Rosanne, breaded and sauteed in butter, flamed with sherry and served with asparagus and Hollandaise sauce. The quality of the veal is not up to standard so avoid the veal Outback and the other veal dishes.

With your entree you receive a delightful dinner salad of garden goodies and a Greek house dressing with feta cheese, sherbet palate cleanser, rice pilaf with raisins/mushrooms or potato of the day (baked is best), apple muffins and breads. Super dessert pastries vary and are premises-made. Table service is pleasant and accomodating; the wine list adequate.

- **HOURS: Wed. thru Sat.: 6:00 p.m.–10:00 p.m.**
  Sun.: Brunch only at 11:00 a.m. to 3:00 p.m.
- **CLOSING DAYS: Mon. & Tues.** • **CREDIT CARDS: MC, V**
- **PARKING: Lot** • **RESERVATIONS: Yes**
- **HANDICAPPED ACCESS: No difficulty**
- **AVERAGE CHECK FOR TWO: $37.00**

Oxford Club

Viscount Suite Hotel
4855 E. Broadway (Swan)
Tucson 745-6500

TUCSON

Quiet and dignified in keeping with the British tradition, this classic dining room offers food for every taste. Decorated in mauve and pink, comfortable armchairs surround tables that are beautifully set. Booths line one wall. Relaxing background music soothes the evening.

The attractive bill of fare offers a plethora of riches and items not commonly seen on Arizona menus. To accent the British image they offer the cornerstone of British nutrition, steak and kidney pie. It is excellent and highly recommended. The chef is also proud of his boullabaisse a la Marseillaise, with a variety of seafood, and a New England clam bake with lobster, clams, mussels, etc. Naturally there is a superb prime rib of beef with horseradish sauce and Yorkshire pudding. The fresh fish of the day is available either broiled, poached, grilled or baked with a variety of sauces: dill, Hollandaise, meuniere, teriyaki, etc. You may also want to check out the roast duckling and the steaks. The tableside prepared spinach and Caesar salads are marvelous.

Entrees come with a choice of soup or a delightful green garden salad. The beautifully presented wine list has moderate prices. The chocolate velvet cream cheese cake for dessert deserves a medal.

- **HOURS: Mon. thru Sun.: 5:00 p.m.–10:00 p.m.**
  Open for lunch
- **CLOSING DAYS: None**
- **RESERVATIONS: Yes**
- **PARKING: Lot and valet**
- **CREDIT CARDS: All**
- **HANDICAPPED ACCESS: No difficulty**
- **AVERAGE CHECK FOR TWO: $40.00**

* * * *Continental*

Palm Court

Scottsdale Conference Resort
7700 E. McCormick Parkway
Scottsdale 991-3400

SCOTTSDALE

With its contemporary southwest decor, this impressive second floor dining room radiates a warm elegance. The dried flower arrangements and the profusion of potted palm greenery contrast beautifully with the off-white walls and draperies.

Evian water is poured and crisp lahvosh served as soon as you are seated. Two or three off-menu dishes are recited and displayed by the formally dressed waiter. The choice a la carte menu is grand and you cannot help but be dazzled by the selections. The lobster Lord Randolph, the rack of lamb a la diablo roasted with English mustard and spices, and the muscovy duckling with fruit sauce reach celestial heights. The fresh fish items are always culinary masterpieces. Even a vegetarian dish has class. Other dishes soar to the same realm. The imperial Caesar and the wilted spinach salads are beautiful. On occasion there is an enjoyable roasted wild boar served with prickly pear cactus sauce. A $39 prix fixe menu is highly recommended.

Table service is superb; the waiters gracious without being fawning. The wine list keeps improving and the showcase storage is impressive. A 15% gratuity is automatically added to your bill. Jackets are required for men.

- **HOURS: Mon. thru Sun.: 5:00 p.m.–10:00 p.m. Open for lunch; brunch on Sunday.**
- **CLOSING DAYS: None**
- **RESERVATIONS: Yes**
- **PARKING: Lot and valet**
- **CREDIT CARDS: All**
- **HANDICAPPED ACCESS: Ramps and elevators**
- **AVERAGE CHECK FOR TWO: $65.00 plus 15%**

International

Paniolo Grill

Biltmore Fashion Park
2594 E. Camelback Road
Phoenix

381-8772

PHOENIX

In the most glitzy shopping center of Phoenix is the latest dining concept created by the owners of RoxSand. It is where the current action is among the trendy set of bons vivants. This bistro hangout is casual, exciting and noisy with an adventurous, far-reaching kitchen. The dining theme is Hawaiian and "paniolo" is Hawaiian for cowboy. The decor is "packing crate" with bare, varnished, knotty pine booths and hard, unupholstered chairs, uncarpeted floors, no tablecloths, and a cowhide and a couple of large, back-lighted metal pineapples on the wall.

The menu is a smaller kissing cousin to RoxSand's famous bill of fare: Kahlua pig, Korean short ribs of beef, Texas chainsaw chili, roasted hoisin game hen, brisket of beef, Portuguese sausage, etc. Along with such entrees you may receive garlic mashed potatoes, Japanese rice, cowboy beans, pickled onions, cole slaw, corn on the cob, etc. There are also salads and sandwiches — including a hamburger. Although very eclectic, it all comes together quite well and the food is good.

Fabulous desserts a la RoxSand are mind boggling. Table service is good but falters a bit when things get busy. The wine list is not as exciting as the food.

- **HOURS: Mon. thru Sun.: 4:00 p.m.–12 midnight**
  Open for breakfast and lunch
- **CLOSING DAYS: None**
- **RESERVATIONS: Yes**
- **PARKING: Lot and valet**
- **CREDIT CARDS: All**
- **HANDICAPPED ACCESS: Escalator and elevator**
- **AVERAGE CHECK FOR TWO: $36.00**

Penelope's

3619 E. Speedway Boulevard (Palo Verde)
Tucson 325-5080

TUCSON

Attention to your dining pleasure is the hallmark of this small haven of haute cuisine. The dozen or so tables are attractively set with rust tablecloths over white tablecloths, candles and fresh flowers. A large wine rack separates the two small rooms and beautiful copper pieces and landscape photography adorn the white walls.

The prix fixe six course dinner is primarily country French with a touch of cuisine from Holland and the Low Countries. The menu is limited and varies weekly. Typically, there are one or two appetizers, two soups, a salad, one or two cheeses, two dessert selections and four to six entrees, including beef, chicken, seafood and "something different" (pheasant, quail, frog legs). In typical French fashion, the salad is served after the entree.

We happily recommend these superb dishes: duck with raspberry sauce, filet mignon bourguignon, and shrimp in a creamy dill sauce. The soups, from the usual (tomato) to the unusual (artichoke, cauliflower) have all been delectable. Salads are more than mere mixed greens, the breads and croissants are wonderful, and the dark chocolate mousse is good.

Service is warm and personal and the wine list is well balanced. Unfortunately, the spartan outside appearance of Penelope's does not do justice to the inside where much good food can be enjoyed.

- **HOURS:** Tues. thru Sun.: 5:30 p.m.–9:30 p.m.
  Open for lunch
- **CLOSING DAYS:** Mon.
- **RESERVATIONS:** Yes
- **PARKING:** Lot in back
- **CREDIT CARDS:** MC, V
- **HANDICAPPED ACCESS:** No difficulty
- **AVERAGE CHECK FOR TWO:** $55.00

Piccadilly Cafeterias

A total of five convenient locations in the Valley of the Sun and one in Tucson. Consult your telephone directory for addresses.

PHOENIX - TEMPE - TUCSON

Eating in a cafeteria cannot be considered "dining." There are rarely cocktails, beer or wine. Cafeterias are fast-eating, noisy places serving bland institutional food. But contrary to most cafeterias, the Piccadilly's serve excellent food — and the price is right. There's nothing elegant or fancy, but it is clean, the food is well prepared and servings are ample.

There are always two soups that vary day to day and are usually quite good. There are over a dozen different salads varying in price from less than 50¢ to over $1.00 each. The servings are small, but you can always take two! Main course selections range from fried cod and sole, baked halibut, red snapper or a seafood casserole to liver with bacon or onions, baked and/or fried chicken, ham and sweet potatoes, grilled steak, chopped sirloin and roast beef. There are always a couple of casseroles. None of the above dishes costs more than $5.25. They have instituted a "Dilly Dish," which is small portions of a special entree and two vegetables for around $3.00.

There are quick refills on coffee and iced tea. During the rush hours (from 5:00 p.m. to 7:30 p.m.) the tables are often not cleared fast enough.

- **HOURS: Mon. thru Sun.: 11:00 a.m.–8:30 p.m.**
Open for lunch
- **CLOSING DAYS: Christmas**
- **RESERVATIONS: No**
- **PARKING: Lots**
- **CREDIT CARDS: None**
- **HANDICAPPED ACCESS: No difficulties**
- **AVERAGE CHECK FOR TWO: $13.00**

Pine Cone Inn

1245 White Spar Road
Prescott 445-2970

PRESCOTT

For 39 years this restaurant has been serving residents and visitors alike. Located in the tall pines you can enjoy dining and music "live" every night in either of two rooms. One has a large bar at one end while the other features the entertainment. Paneling, beamed ceilings and a rough stone wall add a rustic feeling.

Menu offerings include beef, fish (Friday is fish fry night with "all you can eat" for $5.25), pork chops and chicken. The prime rib has always been tasty and memorable and is available Thurs. and Sat. nites. Don't overlook the grilled pork chops, baked ham or the shrimp scampi. Many of the locals swear these are the best in Arizona. All dinners include a promptly served vegetable relish tray, homemade soup (when available, try the corn chowder), an average iceberg lettuce salad and hot biscuits with honey. Our choice of rice was a delightful surprise — a mixture of wild and regular rice. The teriyaki steak is good and done to perfection. Desserts are limited to a couple of fresh, homebaked pies.

There is a nicely balanced wine list as well as house wine. Try the Italian Bottachelli. A children's menu for those under 12 is also available. Reduced price "Early Bird" specials are available from 4–6 p.m. This is a popular place and reservations are a must on the weekends.

- **HOURS: Mon. thru Sun.: 4:00 p.m.–10:30 p.m.**
  Open for breakfast and lunch
- **CLOSING DAYS: Christmas**
- **RESERVATIONS: Yes**
- **PARKING: Lot**
- **CREDIT CARDS: All**
- **HANDICAPPED ACCESS: No difficulty**
- **AVERAGE CHECK FOR TWO: $32.00**

Pinnacle Peak

10426 E. Jomax Rd., Scottsdale 563-5133
6541 E. Tanque Verde Rd., Tucson 296-0911

SCOTTSDALE – TUCSON

Step into jeans and get ready for good home on the range cookin'. The Old West setting of wooden tables, benches and rustic wood beam ceilings will make you smile. If you are looking for attention — men, wear a necktie. A cowgirl waitress will be along and, with much ado, snip your tie off and add it to the thousands of others hanging from the rafters.

The star attractions are cowboy and cowgirl steaks broiled over mesquite. Choices range from a two-pound Porterhouse and T-bones to N.Y. strip and top sirloins. If steak is not for you there is roast chicken, and in Tucson you can try pork ribs or broiled pit beef in a skillet with a choice of four sauces. Included with these hearty entrees are tasty cowboy beans served homestyle, an ordinary iceberg lettuce salad and hot ranch style bread. A baked potato is extra.

Dessert is a good apple pie with cinnamon ice cream. The cheesecake is ho-hum. The paper napkins are a disappointment. The bar hustles up good cocktails, glasses or pitchers of beer, and wines served by the glass.

You can eat inside or out under the stars. There is country-western music every night and at the Scottsdale Pinnacle Peak there is a gun fight melodrama the kids will enjoy.

- **HOURS: Mon. thru Sun.: 4:00 p.m.–11:00 p.m. (Scott.)**
  Mon. thru Sun.: 5:00 p.m.–10:00 p.m. (Tucson)
- **CLOSING DAYS: None**
- **RESERVATIONS: No**
- **PARKING: Lots**
- **CREDIT CARDS: All**
- **HANDICAPPED ACCESS: No difficulty**
- **AVERAGE CHECK FOR TWO: $30.00**

Pointe in Tyme/South Mountain

11111 N. 7th St., Phoenix 866-7500
7777 S. Pointe Pkwy, Phoenix 438-9000

PHOENIX

These are both clubby places with massive stained wood paneling, beams, rafters, a huge pillared mahogany bar, fireplaces and crystal chandliers. A dignified, masculine tone prevails. Old photos on the walls and beveled glass windows evoke yesteryear.

Peach colored napkins, sparkling crystal and dinnerware are picture-perfect at tables and booths. The captain's chairs are small but comfortable. The menu is as diversified as any in the Valley. Each dish is a recipe from a world famous (?) restaurant, and names and locations are noted. Thus, the pasta pescadora, a delicious combination of shrimp, clams, mushrooms in cream sherry sauce over linguini, comes from the Old Bonita Store, Bonita, California; the carpet-bagger steak from Fraunces Tavern, New York City; the nifty lemon chicken from the Red Circle Inn, Nashotah, Wisconsin; and the veal Asca from the Waldorf Astoria in New York City. They have a commendable prime rib that is carved tableside from a special trolley.

Salads are a la carte, the warm, five-grain bread is excellent, but the places can be very noisy. The revolving door at the rest rooms can create confusion. Table service is spotty.

- **HOURS: Mon. thru Sun.: 5:00 p.m.–11:00 p.m.**
  Open for lunch
- **CLOSING DAYS: None**
- **RESERVATIONS: Yes**
- **PARKING: Lots**
- **CREDIT CARDS: All**
- **HANDICAPPED ACCESS: Steps: front door & inside**
- **AVERAGE CHECK FOR TWO: $50.00**

Prego

5816 N. 16th Street (Bethany Home)
Phoenix 241-0288

PHOENIX

This is 16th Street's contribution to Italian cuisine — it is Prego, which means "welcome" in Italian. This is a small place, brightly lit, making good use of mirrors, black and white tile on the floor, tables and chairs but no booths. It evokes a semi-delicatessen atmosphere with a high tech decor. It can be noisy but this is sublimated by some tantalizing food.

The menu ranges through a dozen or so pasta creations, scampi, chicken and veal dishes to a couple of steaks. The Greek and Caesar salads are basic and good. All entrees are served with a choice of a daily soup (usually good but most often minestrone) or an excellent garden salad with a zesty dressing, fresh market vegetables and toasted garlic bread. A fresh fish of the day varies with the season and ocean currents, and is posted on a blackboard.

Among the more exciting and consistent dishes served are rolled veal stuffed with spinach, mushrooms, prosciutto ham and cheese in a wine sauce, and scallops in a basil cream sauce with fettucine. The fettucine Alfredo, the linguini and the tortellini Rosario are also good. The wine list is decent and appropriate for the fare. A dessert tray is presented at meal's end. Table service is inconsistent.

- **HOURS: Mon. thru Sun.: 5:00 p.m.–12:00 midnight**
  Open for lunch
- **CLOSING DAYS: None**
- **RESERVATIONS: Yes**
- **PARKING: Shopping center lot**
- **CREDIT CARDS: All**
- **HANDICAPPED ACCESS: No difficulty**
- **AVERAGE CHECK FOR TWO: $30.00**

Prescott Mining Company

155 Plaza Drive
Prescott 445-1991

PRESCOTT

The Prescott Mining Company has the feeling of a ski lodge from the seasonal open fire to the raftered ceilings. The entrance level has many booths and tables or, with luck, you can dine on the patio overlooking the waterfall and mining memorabilia. Everywhere there are bare wood floors and a very rustic feeling pervades.

The menu is divided into four categories of beef, seafood, veal and chicken plus the Miner's Feast for two, which includes slices of prime rib of beef, king crab legs, broiled breast of chicken and sauteed scallops. The excellent prime rib is available in two cuts, and there are three soups with the cold gazpacho being the best. Dinners include both soup and salad, a good, warm, fresh mini-loaf of bread with butter, and choice of either rice pilaf, baked potato, fettucini pasta or a fresh streamed vegetable.

A suitable finish is their special dessert mud pie — mocha ice cream on a dark chocolate crumb crust topped with thick, sweet fudge and whipped cream. Wow! Other dessert choices do not compare.

The diverse and fairly priced wine list has some good choices. Table service is snappy.

- **HOURS: Sun. thru Thurs.: 5:00 p.m.–10:00 p.m.**
  Fri. and Sat.: 5:00 p.m.–10:30 p.m.
  Open for lunch
- **CLOSING DAYS: None**
- **RESERVATIONS: Yes**
- **PARKING: Lot**
- **CREDIT CARDS: MC, V**
- **HANDICAPPED ACCESS: 5 steps down inside**
- **AVERAGE CHECK FOR TWO: $38.00**

American
Seafood

The Quilted Bear

6316 N. Scottsdale Road (Lincoln)
Scottsdale 948-7760

SCOTTSDALE

Here is a delightful repast amid an array of carved wooden bears and other lovable animals on walls, tables, lamps, etc. White cushioned wicker furniture adds to the comeliness of the decor.

The menu is a melange of culinary offerings (prime rib, steaks, beef liver, crab legs, fried chicken, lamb chops, frozen fish, etc.), plus a choice of three flavorful soups and a top-notch salad bar. This is one of the best salad bars in the Valley. There is fresh, tender spinach (or iceberg lettuce, if you wish), and some 20 different makings including radishes, green pepper, bean sprouts, cauliflower, red cabbage, shrimp, and celery, plus grated cheese, croutons, bacon, sesame seeds, sunflower seeds and wheat germ. There are six zippy dressings, and one is an acceptable diet Italian.

There are always several off-menu fresh fish items, which have been good, and the prime rib usually deserves raves. The steaks disappoint as often as they please. Don't miss the rainbow trout stuffed with crabmeat and shrimp.

Desserts are standard. The wine list is small but sincere, and the table service is well-meaning and friendly.

- **HOURS: Sun. thru Thurs.: 5:00 p.m.–10:30 p.m.**
  Fri. and Sat.: 5:00 p.m.–11:00 p.m.
  Open for breakfast and lunch
- **CLOSING DAYS: None**
- **RESERVATIONS: Yes**
- **PARKING: Lot**
- **CREDIT CARDS: All**
- **HANDICAPPED ACCESS: Four small entrance steps**
- **AVERAGE CHECK FOR TWO: $35.00**

Raffaele's

2999 N. 44th Street, Phoenix 952-0063
2909 S. Dobson Road, Mesa 838-0090

PHOENIX – MESA

Welcome to some of the best Italian cuisine in Arizona. Enjoy the elegance of fine food that nourished the Caesars in two, comfortable, cozy places with special charm and informal conviviality. There are no booths, only tables and chairs with blue and white napery and modest artwork on the walls. Piped in music does not offend.

The balanced menu is not overpowering, but covers the needs of any famished guest. Pasta dishes hit all the highlights with the homemade ravioli and tortellini alla Romana being standouts. Among the veal selections do not overlook the sauteed veal with baby artichokes, capers, white wine and lemon. However, the chef hits his stride with two specialities, grilled homemade sausage on a bed of fettucine dappled with porcini mushrooms and a chicken breast stuffed with scallops, shrimp and sauteed with shallots, brandy, tarragon and cream.

All meals come with excellent buttery, garlic toast, an above average fresh garden salad and steamed vegetable of the day. The Caesar salad is above reproach and is available for one. Waiters recite the dessert list but so far none have impressed. Table service varies from excellent to indifferent. The wine list has been improved and prices are reasonable.

- **HOURS:** Sun. thru Thurs.: 5:00 p.m.–10:00 p.m.
  Fri. and Sat.: 5:00 p.m.–11:00 p.m.
  Open for lunch
- **CLOSING DAYS:** None
- **RESERVATIONS:** Yes
- **PARKING:** Lots and garage
- **CREDIT CARDS:** All
- **HANDICAPPED ACCESS:** No difficulty
- **AVERAGE CHECK FOR TWO:** $34.00

The Ranchers Club

Hotel Park
5151 E. Grant Road (Rosemont)
Tucson   797-2624

TUCSON

The decor and ambience of this striking restaurant-lounge is best described as Southwest Victorian. The mood is relaxing and sedate. It is easy to while away a pleasant evening in the cozy comfort of soft chairs with the enjoyable music of a harpist.

This is the place of really huge steaks, and for a $4 additional charge they encourage you to share a steak with another person and for another $4 even share with a third person. All steaks are grilled with special woods and you choose the grill wood: mesquite, hickory, sassafras or wild cherry. With every main course you get a choice of over 16 butters and sauces to complement your steak. Thus you pick either wild mushroom sauce, bearnaise, curried apple chutney, green chili salsa, gazpacho butter, honey cup mustard, horseradish cream, etc. You also pick two potatos or vegetables from a list of eight.

The steaks are juicy, succulent and taste perfect, and range from rib to porterhouse with all cuts in between. The menu also lists lamb, pork, chicken, veal, lobsters and seafoods, but they do not impress. Salads and soups are a la carte and don't miss the Ranchers Club chocolate tort for dessert.

- **HOURS: Mon. thru Sat.: 5:30 p.m.–10:00 p.m.**
  Open for lunch
- **CLOSING DAYS: Sun.**
- **RESERVATIONS: Yes**
- **PARKING: Hotel lot**
- **CREDIT CARDS: All**
- **HANDICAPPED ACCESS: No difficulty**
- **AVERAGE CHECK FOR TWO: $60.00**

Red Lobster

A total of seven convenient locations in the Valley of the Sun and two in Tucson. Consult your telephone directory for addresses.

PHOENIX – SCTSDL – TEMPE – MESA – TUCSON

It is not luxury dining, but it is good food and the price is right. In keeping with the menu, the decor of the nine dining rooms is coldly nautical with few frills and luxuries. They have added carpeting but there are no tablecloths at booths that line the walls and at tables in the center. The dining areas are well lit, everything is spotlessly clean, and waitress service is quick and nimble even when crowded.

The attraction is hearty seafood combinations of crab legs, scallops, fried shrimp, fish filets, fried oysters, fish fingers, deviled crab, etc. Everything on the menu is frozen, but there are blackboards around the dining rooms that list the fresh fish entrees.

All seafood platters come with an acceptable toasted buttered, bread and your choice of any two of the following: a fresh, well made cole slaw (our favorite), iceberg lettuce salad (choice of dressings), veggie of the day, rice pilaf, applesauce, cottage cheese, a decent baked potato or above average French fried potatoes.

A couple of steaks and a chicken dish are also available. The cocktail list includes some exotic potables and a nice dessert selection is presented on a tray.

- **HOURS: Sun. thru Thurs.: 5:00 p.m.–10:00 p.m.**
Fri. and Sat.: 5:00 p.m.–11:00 p.m.
Open for lunch
- **CLOSING DAYS: None**
- **RESERVATIONS: Yes**
- **PARKING: Lots**
- **CREDIT CARDS: All**
- **HANDICAPPED ACCESS: No difficulty**
- **AVERAGE CHECK FOR TWO: $24.00**

Remington's

Sheraton Scottsdale Resort
7200 N. Scottsdale Road — 948-5000
Scottsdale — 951-5101

SCOTTSDALE

This fancy, plush spot on exclusive Scottsdale Road is distinctive and attractive with dining in or outdoors in an ambience of muted luxury. In three distinct dining areas, lush plants, original works of art, stone columns, fireplaces and an overhead trellis serve to enhance the elegant decor.

The menu is a plethora of riches, and some come over very well while others miss the mark. On the plus side are the grilled sea scallops, chicken diablo with south-western sauce, and the veal chops. The fresh fish of the day and the steaks have never disappointed. However, the tiger prawns and the rack of lamb with Dijon mustard and rosemary both lack excitement. Only fresh vegetables are served with the meal, baked, au gratin or Lyonaise potatoes are $2.25 extra. Salads are a la carte with the field green dinner salad improving; go for the spinach or Caesar salads, which are zippy and nice.

The mediocre desserts are brought to the table on a tray. Coffee comes with an assortment of add-ins: orange peel, rock sugar, chocolate bits, etc. The wine list is basically overpriced. Table service is not as polished as it should be. Piano music from the nearby bar is pleasant and a nice plus.

- **HOURS:** **Sun. thru Thurs.: 5:00 p.m.–10:00 p.m.**
Fri. and Sat.: 5:00 p.m.–10:30 p.m.
Open for lunch
- **CLOSING DAYS: None**
- **RESERVATIONS: Yes**
- **PARKING: Lot and valet**
- **CREDIT CARDS: All**
- **HANDICAPPED ACCESS: No difficulty**
- **AVERAGE CHECK FOR TWO: $58.00**

*

French
American

Rene at Tlaquepaque

Tlaquepaque Village
Highway 179
Sedona 282-9225

SEDONA

Located in a quiet corner of Tlaquepaque, Sedona's special Mexican architectural delight on the banks of Oak Creek, chef Rene oversees food preparation in his immaculate kitchen while Jan, his wife, greets and seats you. The walls of two dining areas are hung with original paintings and prints by some of the most famous southwestern artists. Tables are set with attractive cloths, pewter serving plates and special china.

Service here is excellent; but on a busy night it can be noisy because of poor acoustics. However, the quality of the food makes up for that small negative.

The fresh trout amandine is so well prepared that we hesitate to try other great entrees. When we have, the lamb chops and the Colorado lamb rack for two with chutney and mint jelly have been excellent. The lamb shanks served only on Sunday are fabulous. The veal dishes are good and the New York cut steak au poivre very popular. All entrees include a beverage, excellent French bread, a superlative salad with the herb house dressing being particularly good, and a variety of fresh steamed vegetables. By and large desserts are excellent. The reasonably priced wine list is diverse and supports the meals.

- **HOURS: Mon., Wed. thru Sat.: 5:30 p.m.–10:00 p.m.**
  Sun.: 5:30 p.m.–8:00 p.m.
  Open for lunch six days
- **CLOSING DAYS: Tues. and month of January**
- **RESERVATIONS: Yes**
- **PARKING: Lot** • **CREDIT CARDS: MC, V**
- **HANDICAPPED ACCESS: No difficulty**
- **AVERAGE CHECK FOR TWO: $42.00**

* * * *American*

The Restaurant

Ritz-Carlton Hotel
2401 E. Camelback Road
Phoenix 468-0700

PHOENIX

Here is posh dining in grand style a la Ritz-Carlton. The muted decor is stunning artistry centered around a large flower arrangement. Immaculately set tables with sparkling crystal are spaced for personal comfort and privacy. Luxury pervades the scene. A talented pianist adds a romantic touch.

The inspired menu announces what is basically American cuisine with continental touches, and is changed regularly. The menus average four hot and cold appetizers with seafood gazpacho, seafood ceviche and escargot empanadas being particularly notable. All three salads are divine but the spinach creation with enoki mushrooms, pistachio nuts and prosciutto dressing is our favorite. Entrees are a feast for the eyes and palate. The mahi-mahi with macadamia nuts and banana curry sauce, five-spice shrimp with rice noodles and sesame seed butter, salmon baked in lattice pastry, and the free range chicken breast with goat cheese are seductive treats. Something less creative? Then go for the N.Y. sirlion, grilled lungfish or swordfish.

The warm, premises-baked rolls have improved and table service matches the quality of the food. The dessert presentation is a plethora of riches, and the wine list is superior.

- **HOURS: Mon. thru Sun.: 6:00 p.m.–11:00 p.m.**
  Open for breakfast, lunch; brunch on Sun.
- **CLOSING DAYS: None** • **RESERVATIONS: Yes**
- **PARKING: Lot, valet and garage** • **CREDIT CARDS: All**
- **HANDICAPPED ACCESS: No difficulty**
- **AVERAGE CHECK FOR TWO: $65.00**

Ristorante Pronto

3950 E. Campbell Avenue
Phoenix 956-4049

PHOENIX

Small and intimate — maybe even romantic — is this small restaurant that features Northern Italian food with a magic touch. The arched ceiling dining room with wood paneling, overhead fans and colorful posters of Florence, emanate relaxed cordiality and a sense of well-being. Soft, piped-in music is pleasant.

With the introduction of a new chef who trimmed the menu, there are some bright culinary high spots in addition to the more pedestrian Italian fare. Now you can enjoy fabulous ravioli stuffed with salmon, radicchio and escarole. Likewise Pronto's cannelloni comes stuffed with duck meat, celery and spices. The 3-cheese spinach gnocchi is another wonder. Roast chicken with wine and figs, roast quail with wine and mushrooms, and tender flavorful rabbit with a special bread sauce are all creations rarely seen on Italian menus. All are dazzling epicurean delights. A couple of daily, off-menu items add to the joys.

All entrees are served with a good Italian bread, warm and fresh, and a decent lettuce salad snappy with a perfect vinaigrette. Desserts are standard except for the chef's daily creation, which can be nirvana. The wine list is satisfactory and reasonably priced; table service is winning and professional all the way.

- **HOURS: Mon. thru Sun.: 5:30 p.m.–10:30 p.m.**
  Open for lunch
- **CLOSING DAYS: None**
- **RESERVATIONS: Yes**
- **PARKING: Lot and valet**
- **CREDIT CARDS: All**
- **HANDICAPPED ACCESS: No difficulty**
- **AVERAGE CHECK FOR TWO: $40.00**

Rod's Steak House

301 E. Bill Williams Avenue
Williams 635-2671

WILLIAMS

Nothing fancy or pretentious, just good food served with pride for over 40 years. There are banquettes, tables and captain's chairs on an attractive flagstone floor, a fireplace in the corner. Red drapes and napkins add color.

More than just a good steakhouse, the cute, steer-shaped menu lists calves liver with bacon or onions, golden brown fried chicken, Rocky Mt. rainbow trout and French fried jumbo shrimp. But steak is king and you should plan to go this route. Rod's special steak, either charred or teriyaki, is highly recommended. The club steak, cut from the lean side of the top sirloin, and the strip sirloin are both excellent. All steaks are broiled over mesquite charcoal. Although untested by us, they also serve three cuts of prime rib au jus — ladies, regular and cattlemen's.

All entrees come with a choice of premises-made soup or iceburg lettuce salad, baked or French fried potatoes, hot biscuits and butter. The soup is made fresh daily as are the biscuits. The iceburg lettuce salad deserves no comment but the tomato-based French garlic house dressing is enjoyable. The French fries are great and the baked potato good. Desserts are homebaked. Table service is efficient. If you are there for lunch do not miss the prime rib, BBQ beef sandwich — it's terrific.

- **HOURS: Mon. thru Sun.: 4:00 p.m.–10:00 p.m.**
  Open for lunch
- **CLOSING DAYS: None**
- **RESERVATIONS: Yes**
- **PARKING: Street and lot**
- **CREDIT CARDS: MC, V**
- **HANDICAPPED ACCESS: No difficulty**
- **AVERAGE CHECK FOR TWO: $30.00**

RoxSand

Biltmore Fashion Park
2594 E. Camelback Road
Phoenix 381-0444

PHOENIX

This is a small place serving trans-continental cuisine in comfortable, somewhat spartan surroundings. A bar and dessert display case are on your right as you enter. A mezzanine dining area is reserved for smokers. Noise and clatter on a busy night are major negatives.

Some 10 countries are represented by the ethnic dishes on the one-page, plasticized menu where everything is a la carte. The Kashmiri prawns with shahi pilau and pear chutney are an aromatic taste treat. The same goes for the air dried duck in buckwheat crepes, and the grilled Jamaican jerked rabbit or roast quail stuffed with homemade sausage. Something more pedestrian? Then there is a N.Y. steak with Texas chainsaw sauce, fresh fish items, and rack of lamb with sauce Dijonaise. They also have lamb sausage and a Japanese eggplant pizza — as well as other exotic pizzas with duck, feta cheese, etc.

On the theory that a peek goes further than a dissertation, RoxSand offers a stroll rather than a dessert menu. The stroll is to the front display case where all manner of rich cakes, tarts and crunchy sweets await your choice. The wine list is excellent but table service can be painfully slow at times.

- **HOURS: Mon. thru Sun.: 5:30 p.m.–10:30 p.m.**
  Open for lunch
- **CLOSING DAYS: None**
- **RESERVATIONS: Yes**
- **PARKING: Lot and valet**
- **CREDIT CARDS: All**
- **HANDICAPPED ACCESS: Escalator and elevator**
- **AVERAGE CHECK FOR TWO: $55.00**

Rusty Pelican

9801 N. Black Canyon Hwy., Phoenix 944-9646
1606 W. Baseline Road, Tempe 345-0972

PHOENIX – TEMPE

Enjoy fresh fish in a rustic fisherman's wharf shack that's nautical and nice. Raftered rooms contain plants, brass accents, and nautical memorabilia on rough walls. You can almost smell the salt air.

Some 25 varieties of fresh fish are offered on a special daily menu: perch, catfish, sand dabs, swordfish, halibut, red snapper, salmon, codfish, etc. Of course, there's scallops, clams, king crab, oysters and lobsters. Besides the special menu the regular bill of fare includes four tempting nautical delights we found enjoyable. The calimari steak, which is actually two or three tender filets of lightly breaded and sauteed squid, is a wondrous dish. And both the salmon and clam fettucines are delightful. If shrimp is your idea of grand dining try the cashew shrimp with vegetables. If you do not go for fish then go for the excellent cashew chicken.

Entrees are served with a fresh vegetable and rice. You also receive tasty sourdough bread, and your choice of clam chowder, or a choice of a tossed green or fresh spinach salad with two neat dressings. Table service is good and the wine list offers a nice range at reasonable prices. A reduced price Sunset Dinner menu is in effect from opening until 6:30 p.m.

- **HOURS: Sun. thru Thurs.: 5:00 p.m.–10:30 p.m.**
  Fri. and Sat.: 4:30 p.m.–11:00 p.m.
  Open for lunch
- **CLOSING DAYS: None**
- **RESERVATIONS: Yes**
- **PARKING: Lot**
- **CREDIT CARDS: All**
- **HANDICAPPED ACCESS: Ramps; no difficulty**
- **AVERAGE CHECK FOR TWO: $36.00**

Ruth's Chris Steak House

2201 E. Camelback Road
Phoenix 957-9600

PHOENIX

Located in Anchor Centre you are seated in an ambience of bleached oak and glass, peach-accented plush blue carpeting, and Spanish tile. Ceiling to floor windows provide limited panoramic views of Squaw Peak and Camelback Mountain.

Everything on the bill of fare is a la carte and servings are large. This is the place for the hearty appetite and probably the best steak you have ever eaten. There are only five U.S. Prime steaks offered: N.Y. sirloin strip, two filet mignons, ribeye and a giant porterhouse for two or four. Four salads are available with the Italian being the best. The iceberg lettuce is sublimated by enjoyable artichoke hearts, tomato wedges, black olives, and a daily fresh dressing.

There are seven styles of potatoes with the shoestrings, French fries and baked potatoes being standouts. Both the spinach au gratin or creamed, and the broccoli and cauliflower au gratin are winners on the vegetable list. A nice warm French bread accompanies the meal. All desserts are made on the premises with the bread pudding, apple and pecan pies rating highest. The wine list deserves no special comment. Table service is usually excellent.

- HOURS: **Sun. thru Thurs.: 5:00 p.m.–10:00 p.m.**
  Fri. and Sat.: 5:00 p.m.–10:30 p.m.
  Open for lunch
- CLOSING DAYS: **None**
- RESERVATIONS: **Yes**
- PARKING: **Lot and valet**
- CREDIT CARDS: **All**
- HANDICAPPED ACCESS: **Camelback front door**
- AVERAGE CHECK FOR TWO: **$46.00**

Sand Painter

Sheraton Phoenix Hotel
111 N. Central Avenue (Adams)
Phoenix 257-1525

PHOENIX

Completely redesigned and redecorated the new Sand Painter room is a joy — and the wonderful changes include the kitchen as well. This reborn dining room is brighter and more inviting and now has a cocktail and seafood bar, but these do not intrude on dining. A piano player or piped-in music is pleasant and relaxing.

The inventive menu describes basically American cuisine but leans heavily toward the Southwest. Wide use is made of jicama, jalapeno and other peppers in sauces and dressings. A Mexican influence is also seen with the use of chorizo sausage and salsas. Black bean sauce and goat cheese are also evident. Featured items are the smoked prime rib of beef, filet mignon, a couple of veal and chicken dishes, smoked duck with apple chutney, and grilled shrimp with pearl onions. All of the fresh fish dishes come over particularly well.

All entrees come with a superior mixed green salad with onion slices, raw mushrooms, tomato wedges, etc., potato of the day and fresh vegetable. The breads and dessert pastries are all premises-made. A very sound wine list is offered at good prices. Waiter service can be slow on a busy night.

- **HOURS: Mon., thru Sat.: 5:30 p.m.–11:00 p.m.**
  Open for lunch; brunch on Sunday
- **CLOSING DAYS: Sun.** • **RESERVATIONS: Yes**
- **PARKING: Validated parking in hotel garage**
- **CREDIT CARDS: All**
- **HANDICAPPED ACCESS: No difficulty**
- **AVERAGE CHECK FOR TWO: $43.00**

American

Sandpiper

12535 W. Bell Road
Surprise

583-1100

SURPRISE

This latest edition to the Sun City West collection of restaurants is setting a fast pace for popularity. The light, airy dining room has a crisp, clean look with tables and hard chairs, some comfortable booths and a bit of greenery. In tune with the Sun City crowd, dinner service starts early and prices are reasonable for the quality of the food.

There is a great flexibility to the diverse menu. Four or five daily fresh fish items can be prepared broiled, grilled or poached — your choice. Not only do you choose soup or salad with your entree, but you pick among two or three daily fresh soups and two or three fresh made salads — mixed green, spinach, etc. In choosing entrees the fresh fish and beef dishes are the most satisfying. The roast prime rib of beef is as good as any in Texas. The steaks are tasty, juicy good. However, the pasta and chicken dishes create no excitement. The dessert tray has the usual excesses, but the daily baked special is usually worth a try.

Waiters and waitresses perform efficiently. The wine list features only domestic labels, but prices are reasonable. Breakfast and lunch are served in the adjoining cafe.

- **HOURS: Mon. thru Sun.: 4:00 p.m.–10:00 p.m.**
  Open for breakfast and lunch
- **CLOSING DAYS: None**
- **RESERVATIONS: Yes**
- **PARKING: Lot**
- **CREDIT CARDS: All**
- **HANDICAPPED ACCESS: No difficulty**
- **AVERAGE CHECK FOR TWO: $38.00**

* *Italian*
Continental

Scordato's

4405 W. Speedway, Tucson 624-8946
6335 E. Tanque Verde, Tucson 721-0333

Nestled in the Tucson Mountains lies one of the best Italian restaurants in Tucson. The two attractive blue and gold rooms are warm and inviting and the tuxedo-clad waiters add a touch of formality to this ever popular dining establishment. The new Tanque Verde place is slightly smaller, more casual, has less veal dishes on the menu and is open for lunch.

Because the dinners are large, we hesitate to tempt, but the manicotti appetizer is heavenly and the Scordato salad for two with mixed greens, ricotta cheese, eggs, tomatoes, olives, salami, provolone cheese, garlic croutons and Romano cheese is truly scrumptuous. The entree selections of veal, chicken, seafood, steak and chops are equally enticing. Our favorites are the veal dishes, particularly veal Parmigiana and veal Milanese. However, the locals say the osso buco is the best in Arizona. With each dinner there is a choice of soup or salad, vegetable du jour, spaghetti or potatoes or rice Milanese. There are a number of desserts, but none seem particularly noteworthy except the cassata Sicilian cake.

The wine list is extraordinary. With over 300 selections it is the finest wine collection in Tucson if not Arizona. With such a plethora of riches, decision-making is often difficult. Service is usually excellent.

- **HOURS:** **Tues. thru Sat.: 5:00 p.m.–9:00 p.m.**
  Sun.: 4:00 p.m.–9:00 p.m.
- **CLOSING DAYS: Mon.**
- **RESERVATIONS: Yes**
- **PARKING: Lot**
- **CREDIT CARDS: All**
- **HANDICAPPED ACCESS: Ramps; no difficulty**
- **AVERAGE CHECK FOR TWO: $44.00**

Sesame Inn

A total of five convenient locations in the Valley of the Sun. Consult your telephone directory for addresses.

PHOENIX – SCOTTSDALE

These are splendid restaurants. The decor is bright and fresh with green-tiled moongates opening off the entrance lobby. Lovely oriental china graces linened tables and booths dramatically arranged in a two-tiered dining rooms. Oriental style chairs are comfortable. Plants, greenery and art add tasteful color to the scenes.

The multi-paged menu offers a plethora of Mandarin, Szechuan and Hunan delights. There are family-style dinners, for two or more, which offer a mosaic of Chinese cuisine with dishes harmoniously complementing each other. You can't go wrong here. If you wish to venture a la carte, we encourage sampling of the tangerine beef or the sesame special chicken breast marinated in an exotic sauce, and served with garlic and onion sauce. Something hotter? Try the Yui-Shan spicy chicken with cucumbers and mushrooms served in a hot sauce.

The house special fried rice with shrimp, chicken and pork is preferred over the steamed white rice. For dessert only the sesame cakes passed muster. Table service is available, mechanical and bored. Parking in the small lot at Camelback is often difficult.

- **HOURS: Sun. thru Thurs.: 5:00 p.m.–10:00 p.m.**
Fri. and Sat.: 5:00 p.m.–11:00 p.m.
Open for lunch
- **CLOSING DAYS: None**
- **RESERVATIONS: Yes**
- **PARKING: Lots**
- **CREDIT CARDS: All**
- **HANDICAPPED ACCESS: Entrance step at Camelback**
- **AVERAGE CHECK FOR TWO: $25.00**

Shells

Mountain Shadows Resort
5641 E. Lincoln Drive
Scottsdale 948-7111

SCOTTSDALE

Bright and airy, and decorated in natural tones of mauve, peach and rust, Shells carries a contemporary Southwestern theme. Live miniature fish swim in an illuminated aquarium. Etched glass, natural woods and polished brass complete the picture.

The two-page bill of fare is dignified and a bit unusual. The left page is a standard list of appetizers, salads and light entrees. The top half of the right page is a slip-out sheet that lists the fresh fish of the day. The fresh fish may be prepared steamed, broiled, grilled, fried, poached — even blackened Cajun style. A couple of specialties are worth considering. The veal crab Daniel is delightful with seafood wrapped in veal with a chardonnay sauce, and shrimp fajitas with tomato salsa is a nice treat. Ditto the cheese stuffed swordfish with spinach.

There are three salads offered: a limestone bibb lettuce creation, Caesar and the American salad, a veritable garden of nutritious goodies. A basket of warm rolls, sweet buns, breadsticks and lahvosh accompanies all meals. One or two specialty butters add a nice touch.

Plan on having dessert. There is serious chocolate action on the dessert tray. The wine list is cosmopolitan with modest prices. Table service is usually smooth and polished.

- **HOURS: Mon. thru Sun.: 6:00 p.m.–10:00 p.m.**
- **CLOSING DAYS: None**
- **RESERVATIONS: Yes**
- **PARKING: Lot and valet**
- **CREDIT CARDS: All**
- **HANDICAPPED ACCESS: No difficulty**
- **AVERAGE CHECK FOR TWO: $42.00**

Shogun

12615 N. Tatum Boulevard (Cactus)
Phoenix 953-3264

This oriental dining spot, hidden in a shopping center, continues to be popular and draw crowds to its very complete sushi-sashimi bar. With its booths and tables in a Nipponese setting, and soft music from lotus blossom land, Shogun is a very captivating place. The portions of food are large and prices are reasonable.

There are only eight dinner entrees: sirloin steak, pork, chicken, fish and shrimp. All of these can be combined with tempura for $3.50 more. Included with all entrees is a delicious soybean miso soup, a zesty marinated cucumber-carrot-celery-onion sunomono salad, hot steamed rice, green tea, and shaved ice with fruit and fruit syrup for dessert — like a Sno-Cone.

Most enjoyable is the tempura dinner with shrimp, codfish and fresh vegetables. The composited "sealogs" are a poor substitute for crab. Both chicken dishes are first rate and the pork is acceptable. Although tasty the tough Samarai steak falls short.

The sushi-sashimi bar is not to be missed with over 21 sushi delectables (tuna, sea eel, clam, salmon roe, etc.) and over six sashimi items (yellowtail, squid, octopus, etc.) All have fresh oceanic sparkle. There are only beer and wine available — no cocktails. Table service is adequate.

- **HOURS: Mon. thru Sun.: 5:00 p.m.–10:00 p.m.**
  Open for lunch
- **CLOSING DAYS: None**
- **RESERVATIONS: Yes**
- **PARKING: Shopping center lot**
- **CREDIT CARDS: All**
- **HANDICAPPED ACCESS: No difficulty**
- **AVERAGE CHECK FOR TWO: $30.00**

Shugrue's

2250 W. Hwy. 89A, Sedona 282-2943
1425 McCulloch, Lake Havasu 453-1400

SEDONA – LAKE HAVASU

There are both booths and tables, a large copper fireplace, a high beamed ceiling, modern colors and plant greenery in this charming eatery with an extensive menu offering excellent value for your money. In Lake Havasu City you overlook the Colorado River.

The menu remains a treat to read with beef and seafood offerings as well as specialty ideas. The Malaysian cashew chicken or beef with pea pods, peppers, mushrooms, onions, celery and water chestnuts are big sellers. Shrimp tempura is superb, and the archduke chicken and shrimp topped with a pink peppercorn sherry sauce is worth trying. The fettucine Alfredo is another delight.

All dinners start with a relish tray of fresh veggies and tasty dip. This is followed by homemade soup or an excellent tossed salad served with a small loaf of fresh baked bread, rice, baked or stuffed potato. If you do not try the latter, you have really missed something.

Made on the premises pies and cakes are yummy and the cheesecake is out of this world. A new lighter menu for smaller appetites has been introduced and is a winner. There is also a sprinkling of Mexican dishes and Cajun items with the chicken Rochanbeau ringing the bell. The Sedona locals praise the breakfast.

- **HOURS: Mon. thru Thurs.: 5:00 p.m.–10:00 p.m.**
  Fri. and Sat.: 5:00 p.m.–11:00 p.m.
  Open for breakfast and lunch
- **CLOSING DAYS: None**
- **RESERVATIONS: Yes**
- **PARKING: Lot**
- **CREDIT CARDS: All**
- **HANDICAPPED ACCESS: No difficulty**
- **AVERAGE CHECK FOR TWO: $30.00**

* * *Seafood*

Steamers

Biltmore Fashion Park
2576 E. Camelback Road
Phoenix 956-3631

Here is upscale dining in the high rent district in the most fashionable shopping mall in Phoenix. The decor is only modestly nautical with a laid back unobtrusive air. The scene is light and airy. Booths and banquettes predominate.

The menu is printed daily and reflects the availability of fresh seafood and the chef's culinary whims. There are the expected Manhattan and New England clam chowders, both good, and about a dozen "fresh catches" that come broiled, sauteed or grilled. However, the kitchen hits its stride with items such as grilled Catalina swordfish with pecan, walnut and macadamia butter, mahi-mahi with cheese, Norwegian salmon with orange dill sauce, St. Thomas shrimp with tomato coconut fresca, ad delicium. There are usually several Maryland crab choices, fresh live lobster, a couple of pasta dishes, and a giant clambake for two that includes a little of everything.

All entrees include a great dark green lettuce salad and a basket of excellent, warm assorted rolls and scones. A separate menu lists dessert items. The wine list covers the essentials. Table service by waiters and waitresses is usually excellent. The Early Dining Specials offered between 5:00 and 6:30 p.m. are bargains.

- **HOURS: Mon. thru Sun.: 5:00 p.m.–10:00 p.m.
Open for lunch**
- **CLOSING DAYS: None**
- **RESERVATIONS: Yes**
- **PARKING: Lot and valet**
- **CREDIT CARDS: All**
- **HANDICAPPED ACCESS: Elevator and escalator**
- **AVERAGE CHECK FOR TWO: $46.00**

Swiss
Continental

Swiss Chalet

169 E. Center Street
Wickenburg

WICKENBURG

Family owned and operated with chef Rene in the kitchen and his wife handling the dining room, this classy little place in downtown Wickenburg is spare in decor but rich in skillful food preparation. Red tablecloths add a dash of color to the smallish room; the piped in music is pleasant.

An easy-to-read menu-board is hand written each day to reflect the market availability of the freshest of produce, meats and seafoods. The chef then performs his culinary magic. According to the locals, the grilled trout cannot be beat and any of the five steaks rates high. We have enjoyed the marinated lamb chops with a special sauce, the tender weinerschnitzel and the jumbo shrimp curry. All entrees come with a choice of excellent French fried potatoes, steamed rice or buttered noodles; a good, daily homemade soup or a nice Romaine lettuce salad with a zippy vinaigrette dressing. The warm, whole wheat rolls are average. The fresh fruit tarts are the best of the desserts, although friends have praised the cheese-cake.

The modest wine list covers the basics at reasonable prices. The co-owner-hostess-waitress adds a Gallic charm to the efficiency of her table duties.

- **HOURS: Tues. thru Sun.: 5:30 p.m.–10:00 p.m.**
- **CLOSING DAYS: Mon., and all of Sept.**
- **RESERVATIONS: Yes** • **CREDIT CARDS: MC, V**
- **PARKING: Street and lot**
- **HANDICAPPED ACCESS: No difficulty**
- **AVERAGE CHECK FOR TWO: $34.00**

* * *Continental*

Tack Room

2800 N. Sabino Canyon Road
Tucson 722-2800

TUCSON

Long considered Tucson's premier restaurant, this award-winning southwestern hacienda exudes an elegant western ambience. However, we are sadly noting some slippage in quality and service. The large stone fireplace, high beamed ceilings, wrought-iron chandeliers and lovely hardwood, candlelit tables set the stage for a beautiful dinner.

The initial offering of chilled appetizers (cucumber, eggplant and mixed vegetable relishes) are portents of the cuisine to come. You may be tempted by the oven poached Chilean sea bass with dill-caper cream sauce or Maine lobster fresh from the saltwater aquarium. The vegetables jardiniere, duckling flambe and rack of lamb Sonora are all enticing choices. Although tenderloin of beef en brochette sounds rather pedestrian, it is certain to satisfy the discerning palate.

All dinners include fresh fruit sorbet to cleanse the palate, four gourmet vegetable selections (ranging from broccoli, brussel sprouts, turnips in butter sauce, to glazed carrots) and mouthwatering dill rolls and fruit nut bread from the Tack Room bakery. For dessert resist if you can chocolate cheese pie and French cherry pie a la creme — both old family recipes. The wine list is flawless but table service is erratic.

- **HOURS: Mon. thru Sun.: 6:00 p.m.–9:30 p.m.**
- **CLOSING DAYS: Mon. in summer; two weeks in July**
- **RESERVATIONS: Yes** • **CREDIT CARDS: All**
- **PARKING: Lot**
- **HANDICAPPED ACCESS: No difficulty**
- **AVERAGE CHECK FOR TWO: $60.00**

* *Spanish*

Tapas·Papa·Frita
3213 E. Camelback Road
Phoenix
381-0474

PHOENIX

Little appetizer dishes of meats, seafoods and cheeses have been a custom in Spain for as long as anyone can remember. This is a noble attempt to bring this hallowed tradition of "tapas" to Phoenix, and it succeeds very well. A colorful, bistro atmosphere is created with piped-in Spanish music, waiters wearing black goras with red sashes and kerchiefs, and an open kitchen with a roasting pig on a spit. Olé.

If snacking and nibbling your way through a meal is your idea of dining, then this place is heaven sent. If you wish to go the more standard route, then a full menu of appetizers (tapas), soups, salads, entrees and desserts await your gustatory pleasure. They serve a top notch gazpacho and an interesting peasant garlic soup. Entrees are fascinating: tender rabbit with potato sauce, a braised pork chop with fried almonds and sherry, stuffed partridge with bacon and Rioja sauce, chicken with capers, pimentos, tomatoes and chile peppers. This is solid, basic food but with a special touch.

The hazelnut cheesecake, flan and the chocolate bon-bon are the best desserts. The wine list is a comprehensive selection of Spanish vintages with a couple of California bottles added. Table service is excellent.

- **HOURS: Mon. thru Sun.: 5:00 p.m.–11:00 p.m.**
  Open for lunch
- **CLOSING DAYS: None**
- **RESERVATIONS: Yes**
- **PARKING: Shopping center lot**
- **CREDIT CARDS: All**
- **HANDICAPPED ACCESS: No difficulty**
- **AVERAGE CHECK FOR TWO: $38.00**

Terrace Room

The Wigwam Resort
Indian School Road (Litchfield Rd.)
Litchfield Park 935-3811

LITCHFIELD PARK

This is dining on the sunny side of the Valley of the Sun. Picture windows highlight the recently redecorated dining room and you look out over lawns, gardens and pool area as you enjoy your meal. The well-appointed tables are usually graced with fresh flowers.

The institutional food is now gone and a new contemporary menu has been introduced. Everything is a la carte, and although basically American many of the dishes have a continental bent. Apart from the standard culinary cliches of roast rack of lamb, filet mignon, steaks, prime rib, etc., none deserving criticism, several kitchen creations will tingle your taste buds. The poached scallops with spinach, mushrooms, tomatoes and horseradish sauce, the veal Oscar, and the curried breast of chicken with wild rice are inspired. The fresh fish dishes have never disappointed. All three salads are fresh, attractive and everything hoped for. A bargain priced Twilight Menu is offered from 6:00 to 7:00 p.m.

A potato of the day comes with every meal, and the accompanying warm assorted rolls are marvelous. Desserts are rich and winning. There is an excellent, fairly priced wine list. A jacket and tie are required for men for dinner.

- **HOURS: Mon. thru Sun.: 6:00 p.m.–9:00 p.m.**
  Open for breakfast, lunch; brunch on Sun.
- **CLOSING DAYS: None**
- **RESERVATIONS: Yes**
- **PARKING: Lot and valet**
- **CREDIT CARDS: All**
- **HANDICAPPED ACCESS: Ramps where needed**
- **AVERAGE CHECK FOR TWO: $52.00**

* * *American*

Terraces at Gainey Ranch

7600 Gainey Club Drive
Scottsdale 998-0733

SCOTTSDALE

Large picture windows overlook a lush golf course and the outdoors is brought inside with palm trees and other greenery. Candlelit tables are immaculate with mauve colored tablecloths, sparkling crystal and gold-rimmed English china.

The a la carte menu is American in concept with continental flourishes and is changed every few months. You are tempted with a nice spread of appetizers from the pedestrian to the exotic, and the salads are beautiful to see and taste. The Belgian endive and romaine with crumbled Roquefort cheese, as well as the Caesar and spinach salads are very satisfying.

The entree list is a plethora of riches. You can tantalize over the sauteed breast of duck with a fresh pear sauce, the Arizona mixed grill of Sonoran lamb, cilantro sausage and skewered beef or go plebeian with N.Y. steak or chicken pot pie. But don't overlook the wonderful center cut rack of lamb with Dijon mustard or blackened Cajun style. The dinner rolls are perfect.

Desserts are displayed and are wonderful with the prize winning terrine of chocolate, raspberries and carmel mousse being pluperfect; ditto the creme brulee. The wine list is modest in scope but quality is there, and table service is gracious and attentive.

- **HOURS: Mon. thru Sun.: 5:30 p.m.–9:00 p.m.**
Open for breakfast and lunch
- **CLOSING DAYS: Sun. thru Wed. during summer**
- **RESERVATIONS: Yes** • **CREDIT CARDS: All**
- **PARKING: Lot**
- **HANDICAPPED ACCESS: No difficulty**
- **AVERAGE CHECK FOR TWO: $45.00**

Thumb Butte Room

Sheraton Resort & Conference Center
1500 Highway 69
Prescott 776-1666

PRESCOTT

Hotel dining experiences are often very dull affairs, but gastronomic adventures abound in the innovative Thumb Butte Room. The special treats range from crab enchilada appetizers and baked brie with raspberries and almonds to a seven rib rack of lamb entree and a chicken breast with spiced avocado, provolone cheese and espagnole sauce. If you are just a "meat and potatoes" type, do not despair. There are tender, juicy steaks, veal, lamb and pasta dishes. The fresh fish of the day has always been good, and the succulent prime rib comes in two cuts.

Entrees come with a choice of rice or potato-of-the-day, a mixed lettuce salad with tomatoes or soup of the day. The house salad dressing is a nice creamy ranch. You also receive a good selection of hot rolls and muffins. A nice touch is a short list of "Lite Entrees" of small portions and lower prices. An array of waist-popping desserts is hard to resist. The wine list is modest with corresponding prices. Table service by eager young types varies. A special early dinner menu is a bargain.

The Thumb Butte is an attractive, two-level dining room with booths and tables, and a picture window centered on its namesake mountain. The setting and surroundings are perfect.

- **HOURS:** Mon. thru Sun.: 5:00 p.m.–10:00 p.m. Open for breakfast and lunch; brunch on Sunday
- **CLOSING DAYS:** None
- **RESERVATIONS:** Yes
- **PARKING:** Hotel lot
- **CREDIT CARDS:** All
- **HANDICAPPED ACCESS:** No difficulty
- **AVERAGE CHECK FOR TWO:** $40.00

* * *Italian*

Tomaso's

3225 E. Camelback Rd., Phoenix 956-0836
610 E. Bell Road, Phoenix 866-1906
1954 S. Dobson Road., Mesa 897-0140

PHOENIX – MESA

Tomaso's restaurants represent cozy comfort in a cafe setting of glinting, hard-edged modernity, stark and posh, striking and familiar. At the Bell Road location (called "Tommy Tomaso"), a sidewalk cafe atmosphere is created with red stripped awnings, street lights and signs.

Menus vary a bit and are changed periodically with receipes being exchanged between locations. In total they cover a broad scope of Italian cuisine, plus imaginative gastronomic creations that have no particular regional character. The pasta list is not extensive but is choice with rarities such as rigatoni Smirnoff, tortelli Parma with Swiss chard leaves, fettucine Via Veneto with smoked salmon. The beef, veal, chicken and seafood dishes are dazzling. We have enjoyed scampi al vino bianco, seafood Portofino and chicken Valdostana stuffed with prosciutto and cheese in a wine and mushroom sauce.

With every entree you receive a seasonable vegetable, either soup of the day or an excellent crisp green salad with a zesty oil-vinegar dressing. The complimentary hot bread with garlic butter is sensational and may ruin your meal. The dessert tray is not to be missed. Table service is genial and efficient. The wine list is an extensive mix of Italian and California vintages.

- **HOURS: Mon. thru Sun.: 5:00 p.m.–10:30 p.m.**
  Open for lunch
- **CLOSING DAYS: None**
- **RESERVATIONS: Yes**
- **PARKING: Lots**
- **CREDIT CARDS: All**
- **HANDICAPPED ACCESS: No difficulty**
- **AVERAGE CHECK FOR TWO: $40.00**

*

Top of Hillside Grill

671 Highway 179
Sedona

282-5300

SEDONA

This is the place to enjoy the best views of the red rocks while dining either inside or on an open deck. And the distinguished food is not sublimated by the magnificent views. The creative chef generally brings off the magic of exciting fare, and has wisely limited his repetroire to five daily entrees, four salads, two appetizers and one soup. The single page menu is changed each day.

The Top of Hillside salad that accompanies meals is a fresh toss of romaine lettuce, cucumber and tomato slices, sprouts and crunchy croutons. Premises-made ranch, bleu cheese and raspberry vinaigrette dressings enhance this creation. The Caesar and endive salads are just as exciting. Entrees vary from good to great. The fresh mesquite grilled salmon, ahi tuna and swordfish accented with special sauces are terrific. The lemon fettucine with seafood is not to be missed. However, the prime rib misses the mark and the rack of lamb is inconsistent. The stir fry vegetables that come with entrees are crunchy good. The daily vegetarian entree receives high praise from locals.

The tray of dessert pastries will sorely tempt your resolve, and the wine list is brief but well chosen. Waitress service is conscientious.

- **HOURS: Sun. thru Thurs.: 5:30 p.m.–9:30 p.m.**
  Fri. and Sat.: 5:30 p.m.–10:30 p.m.
  Open for lunch
- **CLOSING DAYS: None**
- **RESERVATIONS: Yes**
- **PARKING: Use upper lot**
- **CREDIT CARDS: MC, V**
- **HANDICAPPED ACCESS: No difficulty from upper lot**
- **AVERAGE CHECK FOR TWO: $42.00**

Top of the Rock

Westcourt in the Buttes
2000 Westcourt Way
Tempe 225-9000

TEMPE

This spectacular dining room is atop a rocky spur in the elbow of the Maricopa Freeway as it passes by Tempe Butte. It is a dome-shaped building with a cocktail lounge on a lower floor and the dining room above giving a magnificent view of Phoenix. Interior cactus gardens bring the desert into the dining room.

The Top of the Rock, spinach and Trumps salads are deserving of awards, but are large and for big appetites. The list of entrees presents a dilemma. How do you choose between roasted Long Island duckling marinated in Courvoisier brandy or Chardonnay wine, crusty chicken stuffed with king crab and Boursin cheese wrapped in a phyllo dough, smoked prime rib, cactus chicken breasts soaked in prickly pear or tequila marinade? All have merit.

A dessert tray is presented by your server with a rich array of pastries. The black bottom pie and two sponge cake creations are the specialities of the house. The wine list is creative and broad with some good labels at fair prices. The serving staff is smartly attired and quite professional. An important negative: the place can be noisy even on a weekday night.

- **HOURS:** Sun. thru Thurs.: 5:00 p.m.–11:00 p.m.
  Fri. and Sat.: 5:00 p.m.–12 midnight
  Open for lunch
- **CLOSING DAYS:** None
- **RESERVATIONS:** Yes
- **PARKING:** Valet and lot
- **CREDIT CARDS:** All
- **HANDICAPPED ACCESS:** Steps inside
- **AVERAGE CHECK FOR TWO:** $65.00

Seafood
American

Trapper's

3815 N. Scottsdale Road (First Street)
Scottsdale 990-9256

SCOTTSDALE

A comfortable, cozy place with original art gracing rustic walls, and green plants adding color to small dining rooms. Green-shaded lamps cast a romantic glow over inviting tables and booths.

Much of the menu is conventional and hum-drum, but some items are inspired. The cream of broccoli soup with cheddar cheese and bacon is great, as is the potato skins appetizer. A recommended special treat is "Our Oscar," medallions of filet mignon topped with asparagus spears, crabmeat and bearnaise sauce. We have never been disappointed in the prime rib, which comes in three cuts, or the fresh broiled salmon. Be sure to ask for the Arizona rice with green pepper in it. The baby pork back ribs, prepared Chicago style, are at least as good as any in Scottsdale. The special daily fresh fish items are always satisfactory.

The Caesar-like, anchovy vinaigrette dressing on the green lettuce salad excites, and the coarse ground, whole wheat bread loaf is always warm and freshly made. They come on strong with desserts. The egg custard with burnt sugar crusting is a wondrous dish as is the home-made mud pie.

The wine list is basically California with a few innocuous European labels added. Table service by fast-stepping waiters and waitresses is good.

- **HOURS: Mon. thru Sun.: 5:30 p.m.–10:00 p.m.**
- **CLOSING DAYS: None**
- **RESERVATIONS: Yes**
- **PARKING: Street**
- **CREDIT CARDS: All**
- **HANDICAPPED ACCESS: No difficulty**
- **AVERAGE CHECK FOR TWO: $38.00**

*

Italian

Tuscany

Camelback Esplanade
2501 E. Camelback Road
Phoenix

381-0515
381-0506

Here is the newest silky-smooth creation of restaurateur, Tommy Maggiore. As expected the food is good, and occasionally great; table service is usually efficient, but often slow; and the setting is enjoyable but usually noisy if you dine inside. Weather permitting outside terrace dining is recommended. Inside, a colorful mural of Florence fills one wall sharing attention with an oak-burning brick oven and a display kitchen.

On being seated toasted garlic fettunta bread is presented, which can easily spoil your appetite for the delights to follow. Pizzas are a big attraction along with nine extravagant pasta dishes. Toppings on the pizzas can include pinenuts, capers, leeks, eggplant, etc., while your pasta can be enjoyed with carmelized garlic, shrimp, capers, raisins, chicken sausage, Tuscan beans and many kinds of cheeses. Dinner entrees include breast of chicken stuffed with spinach, ricotta and gruyere cheeses, oven-roasted rabbit, veal sausage, steaks prepared Florentine style, and grilled fresh fish with olives, capers, etc. The culinary wonders go on and on.

A luscious dessert tray accenting calorie-rich pastries is presented at meal's end. The wine list hits the highlights of Italian and California vineyards with a good range of prices.

- **HOURS:** **Mon. thru Sat.: 5:00 p.m.–12 midnight**
  Open for lunch
- **CLOSING DAYS:** **Sun.**
- **RESERVATIONS:** **Yes**
- **PARKING:** **Lot, valet and garage**
- **CREDIT CARDS:** **All**
- **HANDICAPPED ACCESS:** **No difficulty**
- **AVERAGE CHECK FOR TWO:** **$45.00**

Velvet Turtle

3102 E. Camelback Road
Phoenix 957-7180

PHOENIX

A comfortable restaurant that is continually popular, the Velvet Turtle is muted elegance in pleasant surroundings. Lush palms and luxuriant plants enhance a striking setting. A large, polished wood oval bar is the focal point and seven dining rooms radiate out — each with its own name: the Garden Room with wicker furniture, the Library, the rustic Arizona Room, etc.

The eclectic menu runs the gamut from steaks, prime rib and beef Wellington to veal, chicken, rack of lamb, lobster, three pasta dishes and sauteed calamari. The gazpacho a la Seville is a dream and the chilled cucumber soup deserves honors. The pepper steak is wonderful. The grilled chicken breast with a jalapeno-cilantro butter, and the honey roasted duck or veal with lemon butter and capers are all enjoyable.

With entrees you choose soup, or a top-notch mixed green salad with an outstanding green goddess dressing or a good Caesar salad (tossed tableside), delicious fresh vegetables and crunchy hot bread. Desserts are excellent; the wine list is balanced and select. The Velvet Turtle is erratic. Kitchen integrity and quality vary from superb to mediocre. Table service has improved. Sunset suppers from 5:00 to 6:30 p.m. are bargains.

- **HOURS: Sun. thru Thurs.: 5:00 p.m.–10:00 p.m.**
  Fri. and Sat.: 5:00 p.m.–11:00 p.m.
  Open for lunch
- **CLOSING DAYS: None**
- **RESERVATIONS: Yes**
- **PARKING: Lot**
- **CREDIT CARDS: All**
- **HANDICAPPED ACCESS: No difficulty**
- **AVERAGE CHECK FOR TWO: $40.00**

* * * *American*

Ventana

Loew's Ventana Canyon Resort
7000 N. Resort Drive (Kolb)
Tucson 299-2020

Chic elegance characterizes this distinguished gourmet dining room where Nouvelle American cuisine reigns. Nestled in the Catalina foothills, you look down on the twinkling lights of Tucson. The view is magnetic, and you dine in luxury to the lilting tunes of a harpist.

The menu is an epicure's dream. An insert lists the specials of the day. On being seated chilled Calistoga sparkling water is poured and you are presented a chef's choice pre-appetizer. You can then rhapsodize over bayou crayfish in wine butter or bay scallops in hazelnut and cream sauce, or move to the soups: corn velvet with crab-meat, chilled cucumber-spinach, etc. All are beautiful.

The talents of the chef are confidently stated with grilled quail with roasted garlic sauce and foie gras and a broiled veal chop with forest mushrooms and a divine cognac sauce. There is also a range-fed hen with a pecan crust, roast loin of lamb in whole grain mustard sauce, rack of lamb, steaks (venison and beef) and filet of salmon with sweet ginger crust and dill butter sauce.

The dessert cart is outstanding and the wine list above reproach. Table service by beige-vested waiters in white aprons is professional. This is memorable, fine dining for those special occasions.

- **HOURS: Mon. thru Sun.: 6:00 p.m.–10:30 p.m.**
- **CLOSING DAYS: None**
- **RESERVATIONS: Yes**
- **PARKING: Lot and valet**
- **CREDIT CARDS: All**
- **HANDICAPPED ACCESS: No difficulty**
- **AVERAGE CHECK FOR TWO: $60.00**

* * * *American*

Vincent's on Camelback

3930 E. Camelback Road
Phoenix 224-0225

Suave and sophisticated describes this temple of haute cuisine presenting exquisite American dishes with delectable flair. It is a compact place of three medium-sized rooms with an open kitchen. Artwork on walls, dried flower arrangements and luxury table settings with Petit Fleur china create a mood of modest elegance.

The imaginative menu is changed regularly and is obviously a benchmark for fine dining on Camelback. Choose if you can between curried eggplant soup with apples and pine nuts, smoked salmon with avocado and caper relish, blue crab cake with avocado corn salsa, and three fresh, crisp beautiful salads.

For entrees you are dazzled by grilled sea scallops and shrimp in steamed banana leaves, mesquite grilled lamb chop with parsnip puree and shitake mushrooms, grilled chicken in vinegar sauce, and beef with exotic sauces and dressings. There is even a Heart Smart mini-menu of nine items that notes the calories and cholesterol count. How can you choose? Add to this the chef's specials and a breathtaking dessert trolley. Everything is wholly satisfying and on finishing you know that you have dined in grand style.

Table service is first rate as is the extensive wine list. Vincent Guerithault's is not for the budget-minded, but for this quality prices are not high.

- **HOURS: Mon. thru Sat.: 6:00 p.m.–10:30 p.m.**
  Open for lunch
- **CLOSING DAYS: Sun.**
- **RESERVATIONS: Yes**
- **PARKING: Lot and valet**
- **CREDIT CARDS: All**
- **HANDICAPPED ACCESS: No difficulty**
- **AVERAGE CHECK FOR TWO: $65.00**

* * * *French*

Voltaire

8340 E. McDonald Drive (Granite Reef)
Scottsdale 948-1005

SCOTTSDALE

The friendly and charming atmosphere of candlelight, fine napery and crystal help make the Voltaire a standout. And when you taste the cuisine you'll think you are in Paris! It is a sophisticated retreat of dependable excellence for specialties ranging from the humble soupe a l'oignon to calf sweetbreads sauteed in lemon butter and capers.

The inspired menu has five hors d'oeuvres and three salads. The Caesar salad, which can be ordered for one only, is memorable. The dinner salade verte is a simple toss of mixed lettuce with a zippy vinaigrette or bleu cheese dressings that could not be more perfect.

The medallions of veal with mushrooms and Marsala sauce are as tender as a mother's kiss. The N.Y. steaks and filet mignon are exquisite. The boned chicken Normande with apples and the Long Island duckling with orange sauce are impressive. The sauteed sandabs, rarely seen of Valley menus, prepared in lemon butter with white grapes have real personality. The superb rack of lamb is available for one. Each entree comes with fresh, crunchy vegetables and yummy Dauphine potato puffs.

When the chef has time, the pastry tray can have some sinfully delicious items. The wine list shows judicious selection and the prices are fair. Table service is professional and continental in manner.

- **HOURS: Tues. thru Sat.: 5:30 p.m.–10:00 p.m.**
- **CLOSING DAYS: Sun. & Mon.**
- **RESERVATIONS: Yes**
- **PARKING: Lot**
- **CREDIT CARDS: All**
- **HANDICAPPED ACCESS: No difficulty**
- **AVERAGE CHECK FOR TWO: $46.00**

Western Gold Room

Little America Motel
2515 E. Butler Avenue
Flagstaff 779-2741

FLAGSTAFF

This is enjoyable dining in Flagstaff at an award-winning motel of international fame. Semi-posh eclecticism in both decor and menu provide the allure in this sophisticated restaurant. The immaculate kitchen is on view for your inspection.

The bill of fare covers the spectrum. The tenderloin of beef shish kebob "on the flaming sword" is a house specialty and is served with pride. The tournedos of beef Ferrniere with a mushroom cap and sauce Bordelaise are prepared with skill. Veal Oscar, spring lamb chops, breast of chicken with supreme sauce, pepper steak and prime rib are all commendable. The Caesar salad is beautifully made and worthy of its name.

All dinners include a relish tray; choice of soup, chopped chicken liver, tomato juice, fresh fruit cup, shrimp cocktail or marinated herring; choice of tossed green or jelloed fruit salads; choice of potatoes or rice pilaf; choice of ice creams or sherbets; and finally, a choice of beverages limited to coffee or tea.

Waiter service is genial; the wine list is modest in scope but so are the prices. Piped-in music contributes to the enjoyment of the evening.

- **HOURS: Mon. thru Sun.: 5:00 p.m.–10:00 p.m.**
  Open for buffet lunch; brunch on Sun.
- **CLOSING DAYS: None**
- **RESERVATIONS: No**
- **PARKING: Lot**
- **CREDIT CARDS: All**
- **HANDICAPPED ACCESS: Four steps at entrance**
- **AVERAGE CHECK FOR TWO: $40.00**

* *Italian*

When in Naples

7000 E. Shea Boulevard
Scottsdale 991-6887

SCOTTSDALE

Welcome to another grand dining adventure of Tomaso Maggiore, local restaurateur extraordinaire. This time the accent is on Neopolitan cuisine — at least partially so. The odd-shaped dining room is fresh and cheery with all tables and comfortable chairs. There is a pleasant hustle-bustle about the place. A bar is at one end near the entrance.

The attractive, two-page bill of fare is easy to read and announces some mouth-watering choices. Of 11 pasta dishes (average $11), check out the cannelloni Rossini and the tortellini Principessa. Both are winners. Of the dozen or so entrees (average $14), we note that the chef has a fine touch with the veal dishes, and any seafood lover will rhapsodize over the Gold of Napoli: fresh mussels, clams, conches and squid sauteed with garlic, olive oil and fresh tomato over linguini. All meals come with toasted garlic bread and a good, dark green dinner salad. If you prefer, the Caesar salad is above average — but an extra charge. Desserts are appropriately rich and sumptuous.

Waiter service is generally outstanding. The wine selections neither bore nor impress. Weather permitting outdoor patio dining is available.

- **HOURS: Mon. thru Sun.: 5:30 p.m.–10:00 p.m.
  Open for lunch**
- **CLOSING DAYS: None**
- **RESERVATIONS: Yes**
- **PARKING: Lot and garage**
- **CREDIT CARDS: All**
- **HANDICAPPED ACCESS: No difficulty**
- **AVERAGE CHECK FOR TWO: $36.00**

White Dove

Sheraton Tucson El Conquistador
10000 N. Oracle Road
Tucson 742-7000

TUCSON

Here is elegant dining with a southwestern ambience. The elegant room, recently redecorated, is tastefully appointed with small Gorman prints, silk flower arrangements and fresh flowers. Tables with highbacked chairs are surrounded by booths along the sides of the octagonal room. Pink napery, exquisite stemware and china and a classical guitarist provide the finishing touches.

Attention to detail is evident at the outset when chilled sparkling water is poured and a complimentary salmon mousse is presented. As the dinner progresses, a fruit sorbet is served as a palate cleanser.

Soups and salads to be enjoyed are the gazpacho soup and the salad St. David with Belgian endive and bibb lettuce. The spinach salad, however, lacks zip. The roast rack of lamb cabernet with Dijon mustard, and the triad of veal medallion, lamb chop and venison are both outstanding. The breast duck "Georgia Peach" is flavorful while the Dover sole with spinach has tasted fishy. The vegetables served with each entree are varied and delicious. For dessert there is an assortment of special pastries and ice creams. The wine list is somewhat overpriced. The menu is changed regularly and reduced price "Sundowner Dinners" are offered from 5:30 to 7:00 p.m.

- **HOURS: Mon. thru Sat.: 6:00 p.m.–10:00 p.m.**
  Open for lunch; brunch on Sunday
- **CLOSING DAYS: Sun.**
- **RESERVATIONS: Yes**
- **PARKING: Lot and valet**
- **CREDIT CARDS: All**
- **HANDICAPPED ACCESS: No difficulty**
- **AVERAGE CHECK FOR TWO: $60.00**

Sunday Buffet Brunches

Brunch: a late-morning meal, usually available on Sunday, that serves both as breakfast and lunch.

The proliferation of Sunday Buffet Brunches in recent years is somewhat of an Arizona phenomenon. From less than a half dozen years ago (mostly in the resort hotels), there are now over two dozen available in leading restaurants. And the popularity of this late morning meal, that serves as both breakfast and lunch, continues to increase.

And why not? Where else can you sample and enjoy some of the best, award winning food in Arizona, from appetizers through a variety of salads, hot entrees, rich desserts, fruits, imported cheeses and beverages, for prices ranging from a modest $7.25 to a moderate $18.00? You can indulge to your heart's content — and usually with champagne! These are the serve yourself, all-you-can-eat places, and for the economy minded the buffet brunch is a bargain meal.

Most dining rooms begin serving their Sunday brunch between 10:30 a.m. and 12 noon. We have not attempted to include the menu-type brunches or the character and atmosphere of the various brunch dining rooms. The reader can usually refer to restaurant descriptions on the prior pages. We have, however, rated the brunches by the standard **star rating** system used throughout the guide.

NOTE: Many buffet brunches close during the summer months.

With so many delicious brunches available, Sunday eating has never been so good. See the following pages.

Leading Sunday Buffet Brunches in Arizona

* * *	**ARIZONA BILTMORE** (GOLD ROOM) 24th Street & Missouri, Phoenix	955-6600
*	**BEEF EATERS** 300 W. Camelback Road, Phoenix	264-3838
* * *	**THE BOULDERS** Tom Darlington Drive, Carefree	488-9020
* * *	**CAMELBACK INN** 5402 E. Lincoln Drive, Scottsdale	948-1700
*	**CAMELVIEW-RADISSON RESORT** 7601 E. Indian Bend Rd., Scottsdale	991-2400
*	**CHARLEY BROWN'S** 5350 S. Lakeshore Drive, Tempe	838-6664
* *	**CRESCENT HOTEL** (CHARLIE'S) 2620 W. Dunlap Avenue, Phoenix	943-8200
* *	**DOUBLETREE HOTEL** (CACTUS ROSE) 455 S. Alvernon Way, Tucson	881-4200
*	**EL TORITO** 6200 N. Scottsdale Road, Scottsdale	948-8376
*	**EL TOVAR** Grand Canyon	638-2401
* *	**ETIENNE'S DIFFERENT POINTE OF VIEW** (POINTE AT TAPATIO CLIFFS) 11111 N. 7th Street, Phoenix	866-7500
*	**HILTON PAVILION** 1011 W. Holmes Avenue, Mesa	833-5555

* * *	**HYATT REGENCY** (COMPASS) 2nd Street & Adams, Phoenix	257-1110
* * *	**HYATT REGENCY SCOTTSDALE** (GOLDEN SWAN) 7500 E. Doubletree Ranch Road, Scottsdale	991-3388
* *	**LA POSADA RESORT HOTEL** (GARDEN TERRACE) 4949 E. Lincoln Drive, Paradise Valley	952-0420
*	**LITTLE AMERICA** (WESTERN GOLD ROOM) 2515 E. Butler Avenue, Flagstaff	779-2741
* * *	**LOEW'S VENTANA CANYON RESORT** (CANYON CAFE) 7000 N. Resort Drive, Tucson	299-2020
* * *	**LOS ABRIGADOS** (CANYON ROSE) 160 Portal Lane, Sedona	282-1777
*	**THE OTHER PLACE** (DOBSON RANCH INN) Superstition Freeway & Dobson, Tempe	831-8877
*	**THE OTHER PLACE** (EMBASSY SUITES) 2630 E. Camelback Road, Phoenix	954-0488
*	**THE OTHER PLACE** (FIESTA INN) 2100 S. Priest, Tempe	967-8721
* * *	**PHOENICIAN RESORT** (TERRACE ROOM) 6000 E. Camelback Road, Phoenix	941-8200
* *	**POCO DIABLO RESORT** (WILLOW ROOM) Highway 179 South, Sedona	282-7333
* * *	**RITZ-CARLTON HOTEL** (THE RESTAURANT) 2401 E. Camelback Road, Phoenix	468-0700
* * *	**SCOTTSDALE CONFERENCE RESORT** (PALM COURT) 7700 E. McCormick Parkway, Scottsdale	991-3400
* *	**SCOTTSDALE HILTON** (IRON HORSE) 6333 N. Scottsdale Road, Scottsdale	948-7750

* * *	**SCOTTSDALE PRINCESS RESORT** (MARQUESA) 7575 E. Princess Drive, Scottsdale	585-4848
* *	**SHERATON PHOENIX** (SANDPAINTER) Central Avenue & Adams, Phoenix	257-1525
*	**SHERATON PRESCOTT** (THUMB BUTTE ROOM) 1500 Highway 69, Prescott	776-1666
*	**SHERATON SAN MARCOS** San Marco Place, Chandler	963-6655
* * *	**SHERATON TUCSON** (EL CONQUISTADOR) 10000 N. Oracle Road, Tucson	742-7000
*	**SUMMERFIELD'S** (RAMADA INN) 6850 Main Street, Scottsdale	945-6321
* *	**TRUMPS** (HOTEL WESTCOURT) 10220 N. Metro Parkway, Phoenix	997-5900
* * *	**WESTIN LA PALOMA** (DESERT GARDEN) 3800 E. Sunrise Drive, Tucson	742-6000
* *	**THE WIGWAM** Indian School Road, Litchfield Park	935-3811
* *	**WYNDHAM PARADISE VALLEY RESORT** 5401 N. Scottsdale Road, Scottsdale	947-5400

Index

The 100 Best Restaurants by Cuisine

Catalan

Chinese

Continental

100 Best Restaurants by Location

The 100 Best Restaurants by Quality Rating

*

Not Rated

For Your Friends . . .

This information-packed
guide book makes a perfect gift.

Visitors and new residents to
Arizona will thank you.

Vacationing relatives will appreciate
your thoughtful consideration.

It is an ideal stocking-stuffer
at Christmas.

Business travelers will use
it over and over again.

A.D.M. Company, Inc.
P.O. Box 10462
Phoenix, Arizona 85064-0462

Please send me __________ copies of the *100 BEST RESTAURANTS in Arizona* at $4.95 each, plus sales tax (33¢), postage and handling (92¢). Payment of $6.20 for *each* book must accompany order.

Total amount enclosed $__________.
Make check payable to A.D.M. Company, Inc.

Name ______________________________

Address ______________________________

City ______________ State __________ Zip __________

Comments from Readers . . .

"I believe your book is the best, most accurate guide that I have come upon."

"It really is a must for eating out in the Valley."

". . . found your book a great help."

"We are enjoying it with confidence."

"Your ratings of the local restaurants are extremely good."

"It was a great help in choosing good dining places."

". . . an honest evaluation based on genuine concern for the diner."

". . . write with authority and verve because they know their way around local pantries and kitchens as few others do."

". . . pulls no punches rating the restaurants."

"I shan't bite without it."

". . . an extremely well done job."

". . . and we are enjoying it to the fullest . . ."

". . . I have given away at least 25 copies to friends who visit the Valley."